Third Edition

PROPOSAL WRITING

SAGE HUMAN SERVICES GUIDES

A series of books edited by ARMAND LAUFFER AND CHARLES D. GARVIN.

Third Edition

PROPOSAL WRITING

Effective Grantsmanship

Soraya M. Coley
California State University, Bakersfield

Cynthia A. Scheinberg
Private Practice

Sage Sourcebooks for
the Human Services

SAGE Publications
Los Angeles • London • New Delhi • Singapore

For information:

 SAGE Publications, Inc.
2455 Teller Road
Thousand Oaks, California 91320
E-mail: order@sagepub.com

SAGE Publications India Pvt. Ltd.
B 1/I 1 Mohan Cooperative Industrial Area
Mathura Road, New Delhi 110 044
India

SAGE Publications Ltd.
1 Oliver's Yard
55 City Road
London EC1Y 1SP
United Kingdom

SAGE Publications Asia-Pacific Pte. Ltd.
33 Pekin Street #02-01
Far East Square
Singapore 048763

Printed in the United States of America

Library of Congress Cataloging-in-Publication Data

Coley, Soraya M. (Soraya Moore)
Proposal writing: effective grantsmanship/Soraya M. Coley, Cynthia
A. Scheinberg.—3rd ed.
    p. cm.
Includes bibliographical references and index.
ISBN 978-1-4129-3775-7 (pbk.)
    1. Proposal writing in human services. 2. Social service. I. Scheinberg, Cynthia A.
II. Title.

HV41.C548 2008
658.15′224—dc22

                                        2007002085

This book is printed on acid-free paper.

10 11 10 9 8 7 6 5

Acquisitions Editor:	Kassandra Graves
Editorial Assistant:	Veronica Novak
Production Editor:	Catherine M. Chilton
Copy Editor:	Paula L. Fleming
Typesetter:	C&M Digitals (P) Ltd
Proofreader:	Tracy Marcynzsyn
Indexer:	Sheila Bodell
Cover Designer:	Candice Harman
Marketing Manager:	Thomas Mankowski

CONTENTS

LIST OF FIGURES

LIST OF TABLES

FOREWORD

Grant-getting is now deeply entrenched in the market economy. It is no longer sufficient for human service agencies and other nonprofits to do good work and to do it well—or even to write good proposals. The funding environment changes so rapidly that it is doubtful that your organization is getting all its financial support from the same sources it did in 2000, when the second edition of *Proposal Writing* was published.

Your organization is now competing with a rapidly growing range of nonprofits, for-profit providers, independent contractors, and even public agencies for both funds and clients. This is an environment in which even excellent proposal writing skills are insufficient. Grant writers also need to understand what funders are (or could learn to be) interested in, where the competition is going, and how to locate potential collaborators who can strengthen their proposals.

This is what makes the Coley and Scheinberg third edition so timely. The authors' step-by-step instructions for effective proposal writing reflect an acute awareness of the changing funding environment. A substantial addition to Chapter 2 provides guidance to using the Internet not only to locate potential funders, but also to get clarity on powerful intervention theories, useful databases, and best practices.

Proposal writing and what goes on before, during, and after submission are all part of a professional process of *communication*. Communication implies bringing together; it requires sharing what we have or could have in *common*. Communication, in its fullest sense, is a reciprocal process. A well-written proposal is based on an understanding of this reciprocity. It presumes that the party or parties being communicated with have a set of interests and concerns. The proposal speaks to those interests. It further presumes a response. If the proposal is properly phrased and targeted, the response is likely to be positive, often expressed in the form of a grant or contract award.

The award itself is a form of communication, one that demands a response in terms of action and reporting, often in terms of shared planning and decision making. That may seem like a heavy load to impose on a single document. On the contrary, it is a much more modest load than inexperienced proposal writers (and old-timers like me) are sometimes likely to impose on a proposal. The point is that no proposal should be expected to say everything that could be said. It only needs to say as much as is necessary at a particular point in the exchange or communication process between funders and petitioners.

With these thoughts in mind, I invite you to share an adventure with the authors and your colleagues. Proposal writing, like any form of communication, can open up new avenues of exploration that will lead to new and important discoveries—about ourselves, our programs, and those with whom we work on behalf of people in need.

Armand Lauffer
University of Michigan

PREFACE TO
THE THIRD EDITION

This book is written for both the beginning grant writer who seeks funding for a nonprofit agency's services and programs and for students. In fact, the book was initially conceived while we were teaching program design and proposal writing at California State University, Fullerton. We wanted to demystify the grant-writing process by providing a guide that was as jargon-free and as simple to use as possible. The book is not exhaustive; rather, its focus is on providing a solid foundation. From this foundation, grant writers can fine-tune their grant-writing skills through years of experience. We are pleased to be asked to prepare a third edition of *Proposal Writing*.

The feedback that we receive from those of you who use the book as a text is very gratifying. When several of you were asked to review the book to suggest improvements in this new edition, you provided us with two main messages: 1) We like it as it is—don't mess it up! and 2) Provide more examples. What we like most about this edition is the addition of a Web site where we provide a sample proposal, more examples of need statements and objectives, worksheets to further develop and practice concepts in the book, instructor resources such as a syllabus and exams, and expanded Internet resources. We hope that the changes and additions to the text serve to clarify further concepts that were in the second edition and that our updates reflect changes in the field. As you requested, we have kept the book short and clear.

We are indebted to the following individuals who provided us with thoughtful reviews of the first draft of the third edition: Bari Cornet, University of California, Berkeley; Stephanie Carter-Williams, University of Southern California; Lynn Smithdeal, University of North Carolina, Wilmington; Molly Duggan, Old Dominion University; and, Kate Collie, Stanford University. We have attempted to integrate as many of your suggestions as possible into the text while keeping the book true to its intended "beginning writer" audience.

Funding priorities continue to shift, human service programs continue to come in and out of focus, and community needs continue to grow. If not for the unique people who see these needs and respond, the world would be far worse off. It is a privilege to contribute to the betterment of our society by helping people to obtain funding to help others. Over the years, we have found copies of our little book on Indian reservations, in small rural town libraries, and abroad. In each instance, we were deeply moved to realize that people everywhere were grappling with tenacious social issues and working for change. This book is dedicated to you: the grant writer, change agent, community activist, caring person. May you have the joy of creating a symphony of service and the exhilaration of hearing that symphony played in your community.

We have many people to thank for their support of this third edition, specifically Ron Coley for his unending support; Lietta M. Wood for her encouragement; Dr. Horace Mitchell, President of California State University, Bakersfield, (CSUB) for his support of the completion of the book; and the faculty, staff, and students at CSUB who provided the inspiration for its timely completion. Special gratitude is extended to Elyse Montiel and Julie Stutzman who gave invaluable feedback and ideas for this edition. We appreciate the reviewers who reaffirmed that we were meeting a need in the world of grant writing and fund development. We also thank our editor, Kassie Graves, for her support and patience as we extended the due date to fit our work obligations. Thank you.

To Ron Coley, my husband, who supported me in all stages of this book and who had faith when I faltered, praise and inspiration when I doubted, and love and friendship always.

—S.C.

To my parents, Lucille and Norman Trinkle, and my daughters, Rebecca and Rachel, for their love and support.

—C.S.

1

AN ORIENTATION
TO PROPOSAL WRITING

Chapter topics:

○ Definitions

○ Types of grant applications

○ Components of a proposal

○ The process of submitting a proposal

○ The difference between grants and contracts

○ Organizing the writing

○ Writing for an established organization or a new organization

○ Writing style and format

Welcome to the world of grant writing! Seeking funding for new or ongoing programs and activities remains an essential role of staff at nonprofit agencies as well as educational and health care organizations across the country. As governmental support has waned over the years, grant writing has become even more competitive, requiring even greater skills to present an effective case for funding. This chapter will introduce you to the terminology associated with grant writing, differentiate among the categories of funders, provide a brief synopsis of the components of a proposal, and offer tips on organizing your writing.

DEFINITIONS

A *proposal* is a written document prepared to apply for funding. The individual who prepares the proposal is called a *proposal writer* or *grant writer*. The government, foundation, or corporate resource to whom the proposal is submitted is called a *funder*.

The proposals we address in this book are those prepared by nonprofit organizations to state or federal offices, foundations, and corporations to provide services and programs to children, youth, individuals, and/or families in community, educational, religious, health care, or other similar settings. Proposals may be written for new, continuing, or expanding programs or for aspects of current programs (e.g., staff training).

When an agency receives funding, it is said that they "got a *grant*," while technically speaking, they most likely "got a *contract*." In this book, we will use the everyday convention—we'll help you "write a grant"!

TYPES OF GRANT APPLICATIONS

Grants are available primarily through three types of funding sources: governmental agencies, foundations, and corporations. The following section will help you to understand the different types of applications and where they are located.

Governmental Applications

When a governmental agency has available funds, it issues a *funding announcement*, which provides the information needed to obtain what is usually called a *Request for Applications* (RFA) or *Request for Proposals* (RFP). All kinds of terminology is used, however, including Request for Quote (RFQ), and we recently saw a funder put out an RFS or Request for Services. This RFA/RFP is the application packet containing full instructions and all of the forms needed to submit the proposal.

Funding announcements for the federal government can be found in publications such as the *Federal Register* or at government agencies' home pages. Many governmental offices issue funding announcements, including the Department of Health & Human Services and the Centers for Disease Control. (See Appendix B for Funding Resource Information.)

Foundation Applications

Most not-for-profit foundations have written guidelines for the submission of proposals, which can be obtained through a phone call or letter or from the foundation's home page. Searchable databases on foundations and their missions can be found online at Foundation Center (http://foundation center.org), which produces *The Foundation Directory Online* and *The Foundation Center's Guide to Grantseeking on the Web* (2003 edition); at Guidestar.org (www.guidestar.org), compiled by Philanthropic Research, Inc.; or at Foundations.org (http://foundations.org), supported by the Northern California Community Foundation, Inc., to name a few. Foundations generally receive proposals two to four times per year, but some foundations accept proposals by invitation only. Some foundations focus their work on a local level, others on a regional level (e.g., Southern California), and others nationally. Still others have identified areas of interest (e.g., literacy, children's health, or educational reform). It is beneficial to become acquainted with the foundation staff who are seeking opportunities to fund initiatives or programs that align with the foundation's mission.

Corporate and Corporate Foundation Applications

The range of corporate giving programs is broad, from the small business donation determined by the owner to formally structured corporate foundations with boards of directors and program officers staffing giving efforts. Almost every large corporation has some form of community giving program. In many cases, the company's home page has a direct link to the corporate giving program. One can also get information about corporate giving programs through the company's public affairs office, contact with company employees, brochures in their stores, and public announcements in newspapers, magazines, or at special events. Corporations have written guidelines for their application process and generally receive proposals quarterly.

Both foundations and corporations are apt to have more flexible procedures than governmental agencies in the manner and timing in which applications may be received. You should consult the program's Web site or contact the funder directly.

COMPONENTS OF A PROPOSAL

Proposals are a communication tool that enables the applicant to express to the funder the need of their local community or constituency, the nature and value of the proposed services, and the expertise and capability of the applicant agency. The following sections are standard in most grant proposals, though the proposal format may vary depending upon the type of funder:

1. *Cover Letter, Title Page and/or Abstract:* Introduces the project and agency/ organization to the funder.
2. *Needs Statement (also called the* Problem Statement *or* Case Study*):* Describes the community or setting to be served and the problem or need being addressed by the proposal.
3. *Project Description:* Identifies the project's goals and objectives and provides details about the implementation plan, including the time line to complete project activities. This section often includes a *scope of work* grid of the project delivery plan.
4. *Evaluation Plan:* Explains the measurement procedures that will be used to determine if goals and objectives have been met.
5. *Budget Request:* Itemizes the expenditures of the project and includes a rationale or budget justification for the expenses.
6. *Applicant Capability:* Demonstrates the applicant's past performance and ability to accomplish the proposed project. Often includes an organizational chart.
7. *Future Funding Plans:* Indicates the plan to continue the project beyond the requested funding period.
8. *Letters of Support:* Letters reflecting support for the proposed project from program recipients, community leaders, agencies, schools/universities, or religious organizations.
9. *Memoranda of Understanding:* A written agreement from each of the partners or coapplicant agencies on how they will cooperate, if applicable.
10. *Appendix Materials:* These may include an audited financial statement, insurance documentation, or any other documentation required by the funder.

THE PROCESS OF SUBMITTING A PROPOSAL

Several steps are involved in submitting a proposal. This process is illustrated in Figure 1.1.

Most governmental funders and many foundations require potential applicants to submit a *letter of intent* to apply for funding and bar applicants

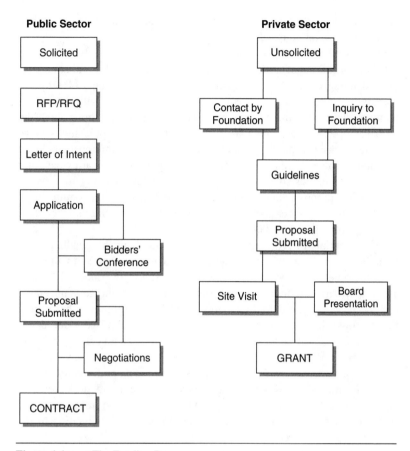

Figure 1.1 The Funding Process

who have not announced their interest in the process from proceeding. Some use the letter of intent to screen potential applicants and ensure the submission of appropriate proposals. You will find this process explained in the funding announcement or in a cover letter supplied by the funder.

In addition to requiring a letter of intent, the federal government often requires that the applicant notify the state government about the funding request they are making. In this case, instructions in the application packet describe whom to contact and when. (This is sometimes called a *single point of contact request* or SPOC.) It may suffice to send a copy of the proposal to the SPOC when the application is submitted to the federal office.

We recommend that you also send a copy to your local legislators so they might advocate on your behalf.

Once you have filed the letter of intent, you will be notified as to the dates and locations of any *bidders' conferences* designed to enhance your understanding of the funder's goals and the specific details of proposal preparation. The bidders' conference provides the funder with the opportunity to clarify the intent of the proposal and answer questions about the proposal in as fair a manner as possible. Prospective applicants receive a written transcript of the proceedings of all of the conferences held by the funder. The conference also provides an opportunity to learn what other agencies are interested in applying for the funding, leading to possible cooperative proposals and allowing an assessment of the competition. Customarily, the funder provides a roster of attendees at the bidders' conference to others in attendance.

The potential funder must receive the proposal by the deadline date. Submission deadlines will be included in the announcement and will determine the time frame for proposal preparation. Many governmental funders allow approximately four to six weeks between the funding announcement and the proposal due date. Foundations and corporations may have more flexible time lines. Funders are very serious about submission due dates, and we are aware of many sad stories of agency personnel getting the grant to the office one minute after the due date and being turned away.

Once the proposal is submitted and has undergone a preliminary review, some funders will make site visits to meet the board and staff members and ensure that the agency is doing what it has indicated in the proposal. In some cases, the agency may be invited to make a presentation to the grantor's board of directors or staff.

The funder usually mails a notification of award to the applicant, and in some cases, contacts the successful applicant in advance by phone. In cases where the application is rejected and the proposal not funded, it is often possible to receive the scoring and reviewers' comments. This feedback is very helpful, and acquiring it is strongly encouraged, for often a grant receives funding after several resubmissions. On occasion, an agency may contest the outcome of the application process. Most governmental funders have a grievance process to follow if the applicant believes an error or oversight has occurred or seeks to contest the determination. Details regarding this process will be found in the RFA/RFP packet.

In the best case, an award letter will arrive indicating that the application was successful and announcing the award amount. Often, this amount is less than applied for, and applicants will enter into negotiations with the funder. During these negotiations, the project description section and the budget section of the proposal will be modified to reflect the level of effort required under the funded amount.

THE DIFFERENCE BETWEEN GRANTS AND CONTRACTS

In the definitions section of this chapter, we provided a simplified definition of a grant. When you deal with a county, state, or federal funder, your successful proposal will most likely result in a contract. Technically speaking, a *grant* is assistance given to an organization or individual to accomplish the stated purposes and objectives. Grants are most often associated with private funders such as foundations or corporations. For example:

- A nonprofit, youth-serving agency receives a grant from a corporation to increase program recipients' knowledge about the dangers of drug and alcohol abuse.
- A health care organization receives funding through a foundation to expand its early diabetes detection and prevention program.

On the other hand, a *contract* represents a procurement or purchase arrangement in which the contracting agency "buys" services from the organization or individual to fulfill the contracting agency's obligations or responsibilities. In this case, the agency becomes an agent of the funder (Lauffer, 1997). Following are examples of contractual arrangements:

- The county government contracts with a nonprofit agency to provide counseling and shelter for abused and neglected children.
- The federal government contracts with a consortium of agencies to provide health care screening and information/education to low-income parents of children under 6 years of age.

Under the contractual arrangement, governmental bodies are legally mandated to provide services for program recipients (e.g., at-risk or abused and neglected children). They must decide whether to provide the services directly, through a public institution, or indirectly, through a nonprofit or for-profit vendor. In the examples above, they have contracted with nonprofit agencies to provide care and/or services. In these instances, those served are considered program recipients of the government, and the contracted agency is required to abide by all governmental mandates. Contracts are a legally binding promise to provide specified services.

In the grant aid examples, the nonprofit agencies received monies to provide services to their program recipients, within their own policies and guidelines. Grant monies can be thought of as "awards in good faith," usually requiring less documentation of programmatic effort over the award's term and more flexibility in daily operations than contracts.

ORGANIZING THE WRITING

The following section is dedicated to the beginning proposal writer and addresses general organization and work habits. Individuals who have written proposals before will be very aware of the obstacles and barriers that typically greet the writer along the way. As most proposals are written under the pressure of deadlines (which are almost always too short), organization becomes critical.

In today's climate, proposals are most often written by more than one person. If the proposal is being written by a collaborative or partnership among two or more nonprofits, the lead agency may provide one administrator and a grant writer, while participating agencies provide one or two other grant writers. If a sole agency is writing the proposal, the grant writing team may consist of a grant writer, an executive director, a program director, and some program staff members. Whatever the configuration, there is usually one main writer. This "point" person pulls the proposal all together into one style, ensures that all of the extra materials are gathered up and included, and makes certain that the grant application is in the format required by the funder. The main writer must read the RFA/RFP carefully and in minute detail.

As many tasks begin to happen simultaneously in the writing process, we can't overemphasize the need for a workspace that allows for the undisturbed storage of materials. Think of what writing a term paper is like— your research is spread out on the table, your drafts are piled up next to it, and your books are spread open on the floor. When writing the proposal, you may have a pile for the data related to the problem; one for work plans from your agency and other agencies, if collaborating; a section for budgets from each of those agencies; and support letters or other documentation from each participating agency. Many people use boxes to contain the components of a project, while others use notebooks.

Even the most experienced grant writers will draw on the assistance of an editor and/or copy editor. In most cases, the editor will be a colleague who has worked with the grant writer in preparing the proposal so that person has familiarity with the project. The editor will help to ensure that the main ideas in the proposal are clearly stated and that the proposal is internally consistent. All of the numerical totals in budgets should be double-checked by the editor as well. Finally, the editor will double-check to ensure that all attachments are included and the proposal is assembled accurately.

We have mentioned that funders impose time lines. However, the grant writer must also be aware of other processes through which the grant application must pass before being ready for submission. Will the board of directors of the agency need to approve the application? How about the boards of directors of partner or collaborating agencies? Organizing a proposal requires an awareness of all of the different time lines that impact the proposal's development.

Investing the time and energy to ensure in advance that adequate supplies for the writing process are available is definitely worthwhile. Purchase extra printer, fax, and copier paper; copier toner and printer ink; stamps and large envelopes; correction fluid; file folders; index cards; pens; and large butterfly clips. Have overnight express mailing preaddressed and stamped in preparation for a last-minute rush. Know where you can go to use a copier if yours breaks at the last minute, and *always* back up your work onto a disk or off-site network or Internet archive. Remember, too, to scan the disk, or attached e-mail files, for viruses every time documents change hands from one writer to another.

Fifty percent of proposals that receive funding are resubmissions that were denied the first time. This statement is not made to discourage you but, rather, to ground you a bit in the reality of the process. Because this business is highly competitive, grant writers learn not to take rejection personally. In fact, too much personal investment in the proposal can work to your disadvantage, as you may lose the objectivity needed to negotiate the proposal, make modifications, or even learn from mistakes.

WRITING FOR AN ESTABLISHED ORGANIZATION OR A NEW ORGANIZATION

Your approach will be vastly different depending on whether you are writing for an established organization or starting a new venture. An established organization has a clear competitive advantage, as it has developed a successful funding track record and established programs and staff. A newly formed nonprofit must overcome its lack of history and results. If you are venturing out for first-time funding, you should consider the following options:

1. Consider linking your program to an existing nonprofit with a similar mission. Meet with the executive director and explore the possible fit. Develop a contractual agreement that spells out your relationship to the company to protect your ideas and employability in the project once funded. Then write the proposal and use the existing agency's track record to reach success.

2. Draw upon the personal resumes of the members of your new team. Involve project staff who have obtained and managed grants or contracts before and use their experience and successes to build a credible foundation for your new entity. You must demonstrate that you have the capacity to manage a grant project and the capability to implement the program you are proposing.

3. Talk to the staff at the foundation you want to work with. Make sure that your ideas are a good fit and that the foundation will consider a "first" proposal.

4. Clearly demonstrate the support for your proposal. You must have solid commitments from partner agencies as well as from the community you intend to serve. This feature is always important but becomes even more so in this case, as you must prove that the intended recipients of the services actually want and will use the services.

5. Have an experienced grant writer review your work. Consult as needed with staff in similar programs. Listen and learn from their experiences and build this knowledge base into the proposal. This effort will demonstrate to the funder that you realize that there are programs similar to yours and that you are willing to learn from them rather than reinvent the wheel.

6. Don't undersell the project and set yourself up for failure and frustration. Use care in developing your budget. You will want to come in "on target" with the budget request. If the budget is unrealistic, you will likely not be considered for funding. Again, seek to consult and obtain actual budget information from a similar agency. Although this information is proprietary, you can find someone who wants to help you succeed and will share, at least in general, budgetary details.

7. Realize that your passion to start something new is both a blessing and a curse. The same enthusiasm that will endear you to some will cause others to shun you, because passionate people often don't listen. Be willing to see your idea morph into something similar but different from the original. Be willing to compromise to reach your goals. Remember, this will be your first program; you can continue to build the dream over time.

If you are writing for an established organization, chances are good that you will be working in a small writing group, or at least will need to obtain pieces of the proposal from others within the organization. We have had good experience using the editing function of word processing programs that allow the user to share documents and track changes. The following ideas may be helpful in guiding the group grant-writing process:

1. Establish the writing time line early in the process and provide due dates to all involved. Make the date earlier than is actually needed to allow time to bring it all together.

2. Establish a tracking calendar for yourself that includes letters of support, grant components, and budgetary items.

3. Ensure that the principal person who will manage the grant is involved in the program design and reviews the budget. This step may seem obvious, but sometimes in a large organization this is overlooked, with dire consequences in the implementation phase.

4. Serve as the primary contact with the potential funder. Channel all questions through you—or through one designated person—so the team doesn't drive the funder nuts calling with questions. Keep a written log of the questions asked and the answers received and share the log with the grant-writing group.

5. Allow enough time in the process to provide a final draft to all involved. This step can help fine-tune the proposal and ensure that you have a great product.

6. Enlist the help of one trusted person and make necessary copies of the proposal. Ensure that the proposal has been copied and collated correctly, bound, and mailed. Keep a copy of the mailing receipt. We recommend using an overnight mail delivery system to send the proposal, both for the tracking ability and for the receipts.

7. Establish a protocol for handing off the project once funded. In larger agencies, there is sometimes a disconnect between the proposal-writing team and the team that implements the funded program. We recommend a kickoff meeting once funding is obtained between the grant writer and project director to communicate funding requirements, reporting requirements, main contacts, and any other relationship information that will be important for the project director to understand. We also suggest that the grant writer continue to track reports required by the funder for at least the first year to ensure that the project manager is fulfilling feedback requirements.

WRITING STYLE AND FORMAT

Although not stated in the RFA/RFP, proposals that are written to governmental funding sources and some large foundations require a formal writing style. However, unlike a research paper in which you use footnotes or endnotes to cite references, references are usually incorporated into the body of the text. For example, one might write: "In 20xx, the birth rate for adolescents ages 15 to 17 in Orange County, California, was 38.5 per thousand (Orange County Health Care Agency)." Or in another example, you might say, "According to a recent study conducted by the Children's Defense Fund (Annual Report, 20xx), latchkey children are at greater risk for stress-related disorders." We hypothesize that this style of referencing developed as a practical response to space restrictions (i.e., with a limited number of pages in which to present a case, you are likely to resist devoting one to references). In proposals in which there is adequate space, we recommend that you use a standard reference style such as that of the American Psychological Association (APA) and attach references.

Formal writing requires that you write to the most intelligent of audiences and eliminate informal references or comments such as "I think" or "it seems to me that." What is stated as fact in the text needs to be referenced as such, and only factual statements should be included. For the most part, the reviewer of the proposal will be a professional in the field who is well educated and experienced in the issue. You will be expected to use professional jargon and use it appropriately.

A proposal prepared for a foundation or corporation will often be much less complex than if prepared for the federal or state government. Some funders may require the proposal to be only three to six pages in length. Typically, the proposal is written in a less technical and more journalistic style, as the reader will more likely be an educated "generalist," not a specialist in the field as in the above example. In these proposals, the writer should avoid the use of professional jargon, as it interferes with the readers' overall understanding.

In all cases, the final proposal should be clean and free of spelling or grammatical errors. It should be visually pleasing with consistent section headers and typeface of a size and font that is easy to read. (Think of the reader who has six of these to evaluate!) Charts, tables, graphs, and other illustrations can enhance the impact of the proposal and are widely used. Avoid using shading or color graphs that do not copy well, as a poor copy will detract from your proposal. (You may insert shaded or color copies into each copy of the proposal, if you think that the funder will not make additional copies to distribute to readers.)

As a final reflection on the "world of grant writing," it is vital that you understand the political and social climate in which you are seeking funding and be aware of changing funding trends. For example, today's funding climate prefers collaborative proposals from human services agencies and educational organizations, in which groups cooperate on achieving desired outcomes, rather than supporting a single agency to address the issue. Also, be aware that while you may feel your approach to the need/problem is the most effective, funders may have different perceptions. Do your homework; review Web sites, annual reports, and other materials to learn about the types of grants and contracts that have been awarded previously. Having a great idea is not enough; you must seek the resources with which to execute that idea, and that requires knowing the funding environment.

2

USING TECHNOLOGY IN PROPOSAL DEVELOPMENT

Chapter topics:

○ The role and use of search engines

○ Review of funders' Web sites

○ Evaluating data and other information

○ Electronic submission of the proposal

Grant writers use technology to access easily information that can aid in the preparation of proposals. Data to substantiate a need, document a problem, or to learn more about prospective funders can all be found through the Internet. This chapter will suggest ways for incorporating technology into the proposal preparation process.

THE ROLE AND USE OF SEARCH ENGINES

Yahoo!, Google . . . these are but a few of the search engines available on the Internet today. As you enter a few key words, thousands of references containing those words pop up on the page. Learning to search the Internet for relevant and reliable information requires a willingness to learn the language of search engines as well as the language of classification for your issue. For example, you might enter "teen pregnancy" into a search engine only to find limited high-quality resources appearing at the top of the search results, while entering "adolescent pregnancy" yields an abundance of quality references. Experiment with a variety of key words until you find the most salient information. Search engines usually supply information on how to use their search protocol most effectively that is well worth reading.

The ability to access thousands of references in a single search will help you to find new treasures such as current data about your issue or new funding opportunities. We recommend that you save the addresses of valuable Web sites on your "Favorites" or "Bookmarks." You can name the sites; for example, Funders, Data on XXX, and Research Articles. Otherwise, it is all too easy to suffer from information overload when conducting searches, and why search for something twice when you've already found it?

One particularly useful Web site to help locate grants and agency management information is GRANTS, ETC. (www.ssw.umich.edu/grantsetc). At this site, you will find listings of funding sources, professional organizations, libraries and data banks, and nonprofit management information.

REVIEW OF FUNDERS' WEB SITES

No matter what kind of funding you seek, one of the best benefits of the Internet is the ability to go to a funder's Web site and learn about that organization or person. You will find information about the type and amount of funding provided, funding priorities, criteria for grant submission, and in some cases a listing of current RFA/RFPs. Looking at corporate Web sites will help you to assess the needs of the corporation in relation to their giving. For example, does the corporation appear to fund high-profile projects, which garner media attention and a high public profile, or does the company tend to give quietly to the community in which it is located? Does its giving tend to promote opportunities to involve their employees through volunteerism? Look for a link on the corporation's home page that directs you to "Community Giving" or to the corporate foundation. If you are unable to find a link to the corporate giving program, use the "Contact Us" link and make an e-mail request for more information.)

While you are at the site, take the time to learn about the corporation or foundation and what it does. How is the business structured? How many facilities does it have? What type of product or service does it offer? Who are its customers? All these data will help you target your proposal effectively, and having a familiarity with the company won't hurt, either, if you are asked to make a presentation to the board or committee to obtain funding.

Corporate Web sites are often the primary contact mechanism for company foundations. Many corporate foundations have online applications for small donations ($1,000 to $5,000). Other funders may require that you submit a brief e-mail request so they can determine your eligibility for more comprehensive funding. Still others will link you to a newsletter or other notification of upcoming funding availability. Requests for donations of product or volunteers can also be made through company Web sites.

EVALUATING DATA AND OTHER INFORMATION

As the Internet becomes a familiar presence in our personal and professional lives, we must also become informed consumers of reliable information and sites. Organizations such as the Center for Nonprofit Management (http://www.cnm.org), The Grantsmanship Center (http://www.tgci.com), and others have databases and other resources that can be useful in navigating the myriad of information sources. For a more detailed description of search engines and using the Internet for research, we recommend an excellent book written by Susan Peterson called *The Grantwriter's Internet Companion* (Sage Publications, 2005).

Some information on the Internet appears to be based on scientific fact, while some is just opinion. This wealth of information requires a degree of discrimination on your part. Which information is reliable? Is this site published by a reputable source, or is it a homemade Web site promoting someone's personal opinion? How can you tell the difference?

To begin with, you will find most valid and useful information on the domains of well-known nonprofit organizations (.org), universities (.edu), and state and federal government offices (.gov). In addition, the following questions will help guide you through the process of identifying a reputable, credible source:

1. Is the article published or not? If it is published, is it in a respected journal? Does the article list references? Do you recognize the author's name or affiliation? There are many opinion articles on the Internet, so beware.
2. Does the site have product advertising or pop-up ads, leading you to believe that the information is most likely posted to promote a particular product or viewpoint?
3. Do you recognize the name of the site as a reputable, trustworthy source for information (e.g., the Red Cross, the United Way, or the Department of Health and Human Services)?
4. Does the site attribute its data to a source (e.g., a study by the Centers for Disease Control and Prevention)? If the site includes no reference as to where the data comes from, be suspicious.

5. Does the Web site look like a quality site? Is it easy to navigate and professional in appearance? Is information about the sponsoring organization or company posted on the site?

Table 2.1 provides some reputable Web sites to assist you in learning how to identify a quality site.

TABLE 2.1   A Sample of Reputable Web Sites

U.S. Department of Education (http://www.ed.gov)
U.S. Department of Health & Human Services (http://www.hhs.gov)
U.S. Department of Health & Human Services GrantsNet (http://www.hhs.gov/grantsnet/)
National Institute of Health (http://www.nih.gov)
Mental Health America (http://www.nmha.org)
National Alliance on Mental Illness (http://www.nami.org)
Centers for Disease Control and Prevention (http://www.cdc.gov)
National Council on the Aging's BenefitsCheckUp (http://www.benefitscheckup.org)
Substance Abuse & Mental Health Services Administration (http://www.samhsa.gov)

ELECTRONIC SUBMISSION OF THE PROPOSAL

Many RFA/RFPs are being issued as online documents. Whenever possible, save the entire document to your computer, give it a new working name, and fill it in. Save an extra copy as a backup in case you have a problem with the first. Some online applications are absolutely horrible to navigate. Usually each section of the proposal has a tab, and the pages are numbered. Most often, the budget pages of these documents are linked to other pages, so an entry on page 15, for example, may change an entry on page 2. The best strategy we have found is to read the form carefully and know how and where information will move within the proposal.

Once the proposal is complete, save it again with its original name, print out a hard copy to review, and if you are satisfied, send it back to the funder. Request an electronic receipt verification through your e-mail software, if possible, or directly from the funder.

If you are unable to take the document sent by the funder and "save as"—in other words, the document must be filled in and filed online as you go—then we recommend that you print out the document first, prepare your answers, and then complete the document. Remember to check spelling. Finally be sure to print the document, date it, and file it where it will be available for reference if needed.

Being able to scan documents to create electronic files of such agency records as audit statements, IRS determination letters, and other hard-copy resources has made the online submission process more streamlined. Many funders will now send their notification of funding, requests for quarterly and annual reports, and other program updates via e-mail to the agency contact. Most funders will also accept any backup materials as attachments to these e-mail reports.

When using technology to communicate with a current or potential funder, always use the polite form of address and maintain a relatively formal, professional interaction. Be sure to include your name, address, and phone number in e-mail correspondence.

3

UNDERSTANDING THE AGENCY, THE COMMUNITY, AND THE FUNDER

Chapter topics:

- Understanding the agency
- Understanding the community
- Understanding the funder

It is helpful to think of the agency, the community, and the funder as each being a mirror. As you hold the proposal up to each of these sectors, different aspects of the mandates of each will be reflected back to you, influencing and shaping the proposal as it unfolds. This chapter will provide a framework for understanding the interrelationship of these three dimensions in conceptualizing your proposal.

UNDERSTANDING THE AGENCY

In most cases, when you receive an RFA/RFP, the funder has stated goals and objectives, or a rationale for funding, which articulates the type of outcomes wanted as a result of the funding. The agency/organization, on the other hand, is seeking funding that matches its mission and services and the needs or problems to be addressed. The better the match between the funder's rationale for funding and the agency's mission and programs, the more likely the project will be funded and the more likely it will be successful.

Every agency's purpose is expressed in a mission statement and reflected back into the community through its programs. Usually, the mission statement is fairly broad or global in nature, identifying the major issue on which the agency focuses and a basic philosophy of how it addresses that issue. The mission statement is dynamic, changing over time to adapt to emerging needs in the community. The mission statement is developed by the board of directors of the agency (in voluntary agencies) or by other governing bodies (in public agencies), which creates policy statements framing the agency's scope and its general approach to a broad problem.

Most agencies have paid staff who turn the legislative body's or the board's vision and less concrete ideas into viable programs that accomplish the mission. In the case of a nonprofit agency, the executive director is responsible for developing the agency's services and implementing them in the community. The executive director is also the link between the board and the staff; therefore, it is vitally important that you work closely with this person or designated administrative staff to develop the proposal.

Reviewing the agency's purpose, its past and current programs, and its future directions is a useful process. The following *survey of the agency* provides a format for examining the agency, for knowing what currently exists, and assessing strengths and weaknesses. The information you obtain through this process will help you to develop a proposal that will move the agency forward with consistency and balance.

Survey of the Agency

- History and mission statement of the agency
- Service area of the agency (geographic area)
- Population served by the agency (program recipients)
- Current programs
- Current staffing of the agency: What is the educational background and experience of key staff? What skill sets are required of staff now?
- Future plans for the agency: Where does the agency see itself in five years?
- Funding sources: Is a variety of funding coming into the agency?
- Other agencies providing similar services: What does the competition look like, and what potential can be found for partnerships or collaboration?
- Capacity to run the new or expanded program: Does existing staff have the knowledge and expertise to manage the new program? Will this program enhance other program offerings in a synergistic manner, or will it compete for resources? Will this program fit within existing management systems?

- Contacts and connections: Do any board members or staff have relationships with potential funders or with political leaders who will support these new services and/or put in a good word for the submission of the application? These relationships may give you access to your audience to talk about your proposal in advance and receive feedback.

After completing this survey, you will have a better understanding of your agency, and you will be able to use this analysis to develop a new or expanded program that provides services in a realistic and manageable manner. Agencies are all at various levels of sophistication, and your proposal must demonstrate an ability to reach a new level of service. Agencies, like any business, can overreach and develop too many products. Too much diversity can lead to system overload and program failure. Consider the following example:

An agency has been providing educational programs to youth in schools and now wants to develop after-school programs for teens. The agency does not have community contacts with youth-serving providers and is, therefore, missing a major resource needed to implement a new program in a new environment. The proposal must allow for the development of this network for the program to be successful.

Finally, the agency staff needs to support the new program idea and want to see the program become a reality. We can all draw upon examples of programs that were sabotaged from within. The staff may need to learn more about the project, be involved in the development of the proposal, and actively engage in the implementation of the program in order to "own" it with enthusiasm.

UNDERSTANDING THE COMMUNITY

Along with assessing the capacity of your agency/organization to achieve the goals and objectives of a new or expanded initiative, you also must demonstrate an understanding of the community in which you will be operating. Programs are usually designed to meet community needs or at least our understanding of those needs. There must be a good fit between program and community for the community to desire and embrace the proposed services. If there is not a good fit, community members will not participate in your program, or they will even fight its implementation until it fails. An awareness of the political and social climate; the issues, needs, and problems faced; and the gaps that exist in addressing them is critical to determining the nature and suitability of your proposed project.

Moreover, the funder will want to know how clear you are about the needs of the community and the target populations and their characteristics. It will want to know whether you can navigate effectively within the community to achieve the stated outcomes. Often, agency/organization directors will test out their ideas with their boards or other community contacts as they conceptualize the needs/problems and shape the proposed project. Chapter 4 will provide a more detailed discussion on understanding the community and conducting a needs assessment

UNDERSTANDING THE FUNDER

Most funding sources also have missions or mandates to follow. In the case of governmental entities, mandates are developed through a legislative process, which also allocates funding to address the need. Corporations and foundations may exist to meet certain needs (e.g., health foundations that came out of the transition from nonprofit to for-profit status). Other corporations may target particular issue areas they want to address such as youth, education, and domestic violence.

Most funders want something in return for their giving. In some cases, their return may be increased visibility and goodwill in a local community; in others, perhaps increased revenue. An example of the latter strategy can be seen in credit card use linked to charitable giving. If you use X card, the charity will receive a percentage of your total purchase. Corporations are likely to view proposals favorably that meet their own internal needs or promote the corporate image in the community. When writing these proposals, be aware of the *WIFM rule* (What's In it For Me?). Design a program showing clear benefits to the corporation as well as the agency/organization but, most importantly, those whom you serve.

Other Funding Considerations

In some cases, foundations may not issue formal RFA/RFAs; instead, they use descriptions of program thrusts for funding consideration and identify those eligible for funding. Foundations give consideration to a well-written proposal but also to other factors in their decision-making processes. We surveyed 164 foundations, and they ranked the following characteristics as the top factors affecting whether an agency gets funded:

- Demonstrates a positive and measurable impact on those being served
- Submits a proposal from a collaborative or partnership
- Indicates a cost-effective operation
- Supports other organizations in the community
- Reflects cultural sensitivity and diversity
- Focuses on primary prevention of the problem
- Has a proven track record
- Establishes new, innovative programs
- Receives funding from other sources
- Has a previous relationship with the foundation
- The reputation of the organization is not too radical
- Has competent, professionally trained staff

In addition, the foundations revealed that two of the most common weaknesses in proposals are (a) not clearly identifying and substantiating a significant problem and (b) a lack of clarity as to how funds will be expended for project activities.

Proposal Scoring

No single approach is used for proposal scoring. Typically, government agencies use a weighting system when reviewing proposals, with various weights or points assigned to each section of the proposal. The review criteria and the weighting system are sometimes described in the agency's program announcements or application packets. Foundations and corporations identify their proposal evaluation criteria through funding announcements but are less likely to indicate the point values assigned to specific proposal sections.

In reviewing the proposal-scoring criteria used by public and private funders supporting human service programs, we found that they generally weighted the proposal sections in the following order:

1. Project approach, including goals, outcomes, and project activities
2. Needs/problem statement
3. Budget
4. Agency capability
5. Evaluation methods

Funders are looking for projects that are realistic, have measurable outcomes with a good chance for success, and are ambitious. It is always attractive if the program reaches beyond known boundaries into unknown or untried arenas, which, if successful, will be a step into the future for the organization (and a nice feather in the cap of the funder).

Many times, one well-placed proposal has a greater possibility of being funded than one scattered indiscriminately to a variety of funders (also known as "shotgunning"). Foundation and corporate development consultants are in contact with one another and are aware of proposals that have been circulated in this manner.

4

PROBLEM- OR NEEDS-BASED PROGRAM DEVELOPMENT

Chapter topics:

○ Understanding the community through data

○ Understanding barriers to service

○ Program design and theoretical orientations

○ Conceptualizing program ideas

○ Working with a collaborative

○ Sustainability and institutionalization

Ideas for proposals start with an awareness of the problems or needs you wish to address. Many times, human service organizations are apt to refer to the "needs" that exist, while funders may use the terminology "problems" that must be remedied. In some instances, a need may be ignored because how it could be met is unclear, or what was once a need may later become a problem due to long-term neglect or nonintervention.

Data can be useful for understanding which group(s) have which need(s) or are experiencing a problem with a high magnitude of concern. Simultaneously, you want to discern whether impediments or barriers to the target participants/community should be considered when designing the program strategy. Additionally, the magnitude of the need or problem may be so great or complex that a single approach is insufficient; instead, collaboration among agencies may be the most effective approach to addressing it. This chapter will discuss these aspects of designing a program and planning how the initiative can be sustained once funding has ended.

UNDERSTANDING THE COMMUNITY THROUGH DATA

Have you ever gone without medical or dental care because you couldn't afford it? Have you seen homeless, mentally ill persons pushing shopping carts through your city streets? These are examples of *community needs*, because they affect the quality of life of the population of a geographic area and each geographic area can have distinctive needs. Other examples include the incidence of HIV infection, the number of babies born with birth defects, the number of persons who go to bed hungry, the number of high school dropouts, the incidence of domestic violence or date rape, and the quality of air or water. In short, a problem in the community requires attention, and this problem is expressed as a need.

An essential first step in determining the focus of your program is to assess the needs of the community and what resources it has that could support your efforts to address the problem. To document community need (i.e., to show research, demographic data, or other evidence that the problem exists), the grant writer may conduct primary research as well as locate various existing data. The following data collection categories will provide you with a guide to the kind of data useful in both developing programmatic ideas and writing the need statement:

- Data on the incidence of the needs/problem, including whether the need has increased, decreased, or remained the same; clients' current physical, emotional, social, and/or economic status
- Data depicting the factors contributing to or causing the problem and data on related problems
- Data comparing the need in your target area with that in other cities, in other counties, around your state, and in other states
- Data on the short- and/or long-term consequences of no intervention, including cost analysis if available
- Data on the activities and outcomes of other organizations responding to the same or similar need
- Data evidencing a demand for service, including waiting lists, requests for service, lack of culturally appropriate services, and costs for those needing the service
- Data from experts in the field, including research studies on effective intervention strategies and evaluation results

The following sections will help you to identify sources for these types of data.

Client/Community Needs Assessment

A needs assessment gathers information about the client's/community's perception of the problem and needs. This type of assessment is usually conducted through interviews with program recipients, focus groups, or questionnaires. Many agencies have conducted needs assessments and may be able to share the results with you. For example, a local health care council or a United Way might provide useful data. These documents are invaluable to making a case for your project. If you conduct an assessment on your own, it is important to involve the entire range of the population that experiences the problem and will benefit from the proposed program (*stakeholders*), including members of various ethnic groups, as well as individuals who serve this population. This inevitably leads to different perspectives on the problem and provides you with varying solutions to serve the population effectively.

City, County, and State Demographic Data

Most county governments and universities compile information about the residents of geographic areas based on census data. This demographic data provides such information as the number of single-parent households, income level and distribution, the number of children, educational level, and housing density. Some university-based research centers have "geo-mapping" (geographic information systems) capabilities that allow a user to define a geographic area and extract demographic data and other indicators for that region.

Specific problems or issues are often tracked by county governments and by state departments working in those issue areas. Teen pregnancy rates, for example, may be found at the county health care agency, child abuse rates at the county department of social services. Community-based organizations will frequently have data already compiled on certain problems. The most organized of these agencies will have the incidence of the problem at the local level (city and/or county), the state level, and the national level. It is frequently necessary to determine how your geographic area's needs compare to those of other areas.

Journal Articles

A rich storehouse of information is available in scientific journals. You will find research into the causes of problems as well as on effective solutions. Journal articles will help provide the grant writer with the rationale required for a particular program design, with program ideas, and with evaluation strategies. In addition, the bibliographies in the articles in academic journals can help a newcomer to a particular field find other important work quickly. Many journals are now accessible through the Internet.

Local Newspapers

Articles in local newspapers can help the grant writer to develop a sense of the community's perception of the problem and of local resources. The grant writer must be cautioned not to depend solely on newspaper reports, as their articles are only as accurate as their sources.

UNDERSTANDING BARRIERS TO SERVICE

An individual whose quality of life has been impaired by a disease process most often sees improvement once they obtain treatment. When, for example, a child is treated for a painful ear infection, the child feels better, the parents are happy their child is well again and the primary caregiver can return to work, and the teacher may remark that the child is doing much better in school. These are examples of outcomes resulting from medical intervention. The ability to recognize and state program-recipient outcomes will be very important for the development of the evaluation section of the proposal.

However, the child may not have seen a doctor sooner to resolve the painful infection for several reasons. Perhaps the parents lacked the financial resources to pay for a visit to the doctor, or maybe they had no transportation to the clinic. Perhaps they spoke a language other than English and feared they would not be understood. The reasons why a client does not access service are known as *barriers to service.*

Barriers may exist as a result of a client's orientation to services wherein the client lacks the knowledge, desire, or skills necessary to seek treatment or prevent a problem. An example of this type of barrier exists in drug treatment services when the client is in denial about a problem. The client may also hold attitudes or beliefs that are not compatible with seeking certain types of services. For example, an individual who uses traditional cultural healers may not value the services offered by Western doctors. Many times, however, unintentional barriers are created by the service providers themselves or through the program's design. These are usually assessed in five domains:

1. *Availability:* Services may not be provided in the community, or the cost may be prohibitive. Are the hours of operation convenient for the client?

2. *Accessibility:* Can the client get to the site? Does it take special physical needs into consideration, such as supplying access for people in wheelchairs? Is there transportation to and from the site? Do any eligibility criteria influence accessibility? To what extent are multiple services provided at a convenient single location?
3. *Acceptability:* Is the service pleasing to the client? Is the staff perceived as friendly, professional, competent, and helpful? Is the decor and design of the service setting inviting to and respectful of the client? Are the services in the client's language and sensitive to cultural issues?
4. *Appropriateness:* Is this service the right one for the client? Is the service within the scope of the provider's ability and/or range of practice? Will this service address the problem it is advertised to address?
5. *Adequacy:* Is the service sufficient in amount to meet the community's needs? Are services as comprehensive as possible?

PROGRAM DESIGN AND THEORETICAL ORIENTATIONS

But what about those troubling behaviors or situations upon which a shot or medication has no impact? Domestic violence, teen pregnancy, elder abuse, substance abuse, homelessness, and illiteracy, to name just a few of many social issues, don't respond to one-dimensional solutions. How does one go about proposing a solution to these problems? Often one implicitly or explicitly begins with theoretical frameworks, which emerge from research and practice and help us to understand causes and posit possible solutions. Such frameworks identify the factors contributing to the problems and how they interrelate, depending upon certain conditions and/or client/community characteristics.

The theory about how your proposed intervention will achieve the desired results is your *theory of change* or *intervention theory.* Your theory of change stems from the information you compile, which convinces you of the best approaches to address the primary causes or factors contributing to the problem or need. Different approaches to addressing the same problem often stem from different views or different theoretical frameworks. In conceptualizing program ideas, time should be spent reflecting on the outcomes you desire, the reasons for the success achieved by others, and the underlying assumptions about what you believe are the causes or contributing factors. One should be able to connect logically the proposed outcomes with the proposed solutions and, ultimately, the underlying causes.

Over the years, the multiplicity of underlying factors contributing to needs or problems has been recognized. Rarely is there one precipitating factor. Agencies/organizations acknowledge the need and will often seek integrated solutions. Thus, while an agency may proffer a single solution, success may not be sustainable across different groups until a combination of strategies is used. This reality points to the benefits of a collaborative approach, which will be discussed later in this chapter.

Service Delivery Models

In addition to having various theoretical orientations, programs can be built in many different ways. These strategies are referred to as *service delivery models*. Most programs are designed to include both direct services and indirect services. Examples of direct services include education, counseling, mentoring, and case management. Examples of indirect services include evaluation, data management, and materials development. Based on these examples, you can see that the term *direct services* implies client or participant contact. On the other hand, when client/participant contact occurs in evaluation through interviews or focus groups, it is considered an indirect service, because no service is being delivered to the client/participant.

CONCEPTUALIZING PROGRAM IDEAS

This chapter has helped you to think about developing a program with the client or program recipient foremost in your mind. It has also challenged you to look beyond your own ideas about what might be a good program idea to the scientific and professional practice literature. With this in mind, we have outlined the following nine-step process to help you to develop your program and provide the foundation for writing the full proposal:

1. *Understand the Problem/Need:* What is the problem? Why is this a problem? Who is experiencing the problem? What factors contribute to it?
2. *Brainstorm Solutions:* Think creatively and freely about what might be done to address this problem. Dream of what might be possible and effective in creating change and positive results. Consider what strengths and resources within your target population and the community can be leveraged to achieve results.
3. *Select Solutions:* Identify the best program ideas from your list. Develop a succinct statement of your "theory of change," or how proposed solutions will lead to the expected outcome.
4. *Describe Expected Results and Benefits:* What will be the goals and the outcomes from the program recipients' perspectives, both short- and long-term? How will the community benefit?
5. *Think About Barriers:* What will keep this program from being successful? Is the agency prepared to deliver these services? Are any broader service

delivery barriers present, such as regulations related to sharing client information? Can you find a way to solve these problems? Would linkage to other agencies address these barriers?

6. *Determine Tasks to Accomplish Solutions:* What major activities are needed to implement the program (e.g., scheduling contacts, staffing, curriculum development, site procurement, and so on).

7. *Estimate Resources Needed:* Consider both human and monetary resources. What skills will be needed to implement this project? What will it cost? What other groups need to be involved? Are resources sufficient to achieve the desired outcomes? What are the community's assets or strengths?

8. *Make Necessary Adjustments to Solutions and Benefits:* Often, we think up programs that cost more than the available funding, or we find an insurmountable barrier or other problem in implementation. We then must make some adjustments to the project.

9. *Identify Measurement of Outcomes:* How will we measure success? What evidence is needed to determine whether we have been successful? (We will address this aspect of proposal writing in Chapter 6.)

An Example

The following example illustrates how program development, theoretical orientations, and service delivery strategies come together. Let's say that I want to design a teen pregnancy prevention program for young adolescents. I am aware of the fact that adolescence is a developmental period in which peers have a significant influence upon my client. In the professional literature, I find that social learning theory is effective in addressing peer pressure and social norms. I select a curriculum developed on the principles of social learning theory, and I design my program to include traditional classroom instruction, a teen theater component, a parent education component to improve parent and child communication, and a community advocacy component to address social norms promulgated through advertising and the media.

Then, as I am reading the program evaluation literature, I find the types of activities that have been used in the past and their success rate. Suppose that I learn that the classroom educational component is more effective when provided by college-age adults as compared to teens or older adults, and consequently, I choose to design my educational intervention using college-age students. In this case, I can be said to be following *best practices*, in that I am combining a sound theoretical orientation with a proven service delivery plan. With this approach, I am most likely to succeed.

WORKING WITH A COLLABORATIVE

The term *collaborative* refers to cooperative partnerships and liaisons for service delivery. In the past, agencies provided a set of services to their identified client base, usually across large geographical areas. While these services were vital and necessary, they often were not sufficient to address the problem fully or meet the complex needs of the client. Furthermore, with agencies working in relative isolation from one another, it was difficult to know all the services that were being provided and their total cost. Thus, the collaborative service model was born out of the community need for (a) better coordinated and efficient services, (b) addressing multiple and complex problems, (c) cost-effective services, and (d) more easily accessible services.

Beginning in the 1990s and continuing today, corporate mergers became common in both the public and private sectors in an effort to bring escalating costs under control and to add value to products and services. Many nonprofit agencies either closed their doors during this difficult time or merged with other agencies. Agencies and funders began to look for new ways to deliver services more economically and efficiently as well as with more accountability for results. It became common to hear funders use the term *outcomes-driven* or state that "It is no longer good enough to do good in our communities. We have limited resources, and we need to know what works. And we must work together."

With federal and state governments releasing more monies to the counties as pass-through funding, most counties have chosen to meet the needs of the public through linkages with both public and private entities. In turn, new partnerships and collaborations have been developed on the local level to meet the needs of clients and funders alike.

In the collaborative model, communities are redefined to reflect better the actual interactive units of individuals (e.g., a religious community, a school community, or a particular neighborhood) rather than being defined by broad geographical boundaries (e.g., the Rural County community or the Major City Community). Service hubs located within the smaller community are created with an overarching vision of one-stop shopping for program recipients. These hubs are sometimes referred to as "family resource centers." Agencies bring their services to the family resource center and forge linkages with the community surrounding the center.

As you can imagine, collaboratives can be structured in many different ways. The illustration in Figure 4.1 shows how service providers can work out of a single location that provides one-stop shopping for clients. Figure 4.2

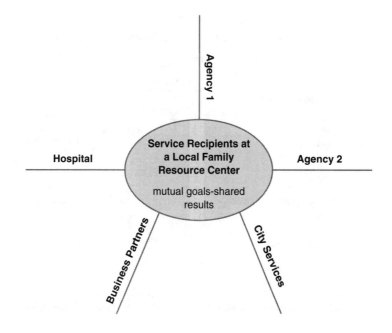

Figure 4.1   Collaborative Model Using a Single Site for Service Delivery

demonstrates a collaborative serving a large geographic area with services linked to school sites and community sites. In this case, the client receives services at a neighborhood facility, and the collaborative providers take their services from place to place.

As with any service delivery strategy, collaboration has both advantages and challenges. The advantages include the following:

- Better knowledge of what services exist in a given area and what services are needed (service gaps)
- More effective in meeting the interrelated and multiple needs of program recipients
- More partnering between agencies, resulting in new and creative service delivery plans (e.g., the nutrition education classes of one agency may be linked to the parenting education classes of another)
- Evaluation of the collaborative-as-a-whole, providing the opportunity to see what difference multiple services make to a single program recipient
- Increased access to program recipients

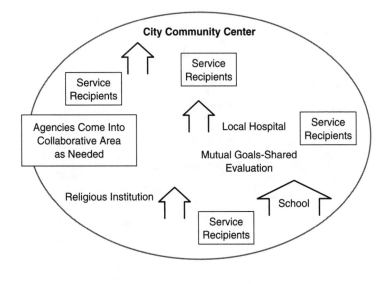

Figure 4.2   Collaborative Model Using Multiple Sites for Service Delivery

- Increased ability to track the total amount of financial resources in a given geographic area
- The development of personal relationships among providers to facilitate referrals
- Increased participation of the program recipient in service delivery planning
- Increased access to local data (studies conducted by agencies or schools) and sharing of past proposals to help write the need statements for current proposals

The challenges of collaboration include the following:

- Significant time spent in planning and at meetings.
- Some funding structures that are not yet adapted to fund collaboratives with flexibility
- Potential problems between agencies regarding service planning and delivery structures
- Sharing resources and taking shared responsibility for a mutual set of outcomes
- Cost reimbursement issues if the lead agency is too small to manage the budget

Collaboratives are living partnerships of people and bureaucracies. To be successful, the collaborative must have a shared vision, mutually developed goals, trust in the word of its leadership, a broad representation of collaborative members at the leadership level, and the ability to select and change leadership if necessary. Furthermore, the collaborative involves community members who receive services in important aspects of its functioning. According to Sid Gardner in *Beyond Collaboration to Results* (1999, p. 71): "A successful collaborative must, almost by definition, have the capacity to tap the energies and resources of the community beyond the budgets of its members."

Writing a Proposal for a Collaborative

When writing a proposal for a collaborative, the grant writer should be intimately involved in all phases of development to facilitate an understanding of the many aspects of the project and capture the richness of the effort. In some cases, the grant writer may be called upon to help develop the project and the proposal. One of the authors led a large collaborative for eight years and has developed a model for conceptualizing proposals in a large group. The following provides a brief summary of the three-part model that the grant writer can use to help the collaborative members organize their thoughts and services prior to writing.

Phase I: Determining the Need and Establishing Goals

In this phase, program recipients and service providers define the needs. At one meeting all together or through several smaller meetings, the community and service providers create goals and place needs under the appropriate goal. For example, immunizations and dental care may be needed in a community that also has a concern about gang violence. Two goals could be developed: one goal addressing the health and mental health needs of children, the second addressing community safety. The committee can make as many goals as it chooses or use the goals provided by the funder under which local services can be organized. Once the goals are completed and needs fit underneath, the committees are asked to rank the community needs from *most important to address now* to *less important to address now*. The definition and ranking of needs will help determine the asset allocation to follow.

Phase II: Exploring Possible Program Offerings and Benefits

In this phase, service providers propose what they want to do to address the needs, indicate under which goal area the program fits, identify expected results and benefits, develop a budget, and provide a rationale for using this approach. In other words, are there any data or research to document how effective their approach might be in reducing or eliminating the problem?

Phase III: Developing the Final Program and Budget

The program offerings are listed under goal areas. The amount of funding requested is placed alongside each program offering. The column is totaled, and invariably, the budget needed exceeds the funder's allocation. Using the ranking system developed by the community and service providers, the whole group makes decisions about what stays as proposed, what might be adjusted, and what is eliminated from the proposal.

This process allows true collaboration to occur. In many instances, agencies can contribute some services *in-kind*, meaning that they will not receive money for these services but instead will pay for the services they are tying into the proposal. (By the way, some funders require a certain percentage of the proposal be in-kind contributions. We will address this issue further in Chapter 8.) Furthermore, in this model, all agencies are part of the decision-making process with the lead agency serving as a facilitator.

SUSTAINABILITY AND INSTITUTIONALIZATION

While your immediate goal is to obtain funding for your program or initiative, funders will also request that you address within the proposal what will happen to the program once they discontinue funding. The typical question is "Do you plan to continue this project in the future? If so, how do you plan to fund it?"

In the majority of cases, the answer to the first question will be "yes," followed by a brief description of how the program may be developed in the future, what major changes may occur in program format, and what new opportunities may be on the horizon. The answer to the second question may be more problematic for the grant writer. Human nature being what it is, we are more likely to have fixed our minds on obtaining the initial funding for the project rather than on how to fund the project beyond the current request.

If you view the question from the funder's perspective, however, you will realize the wisdom of this inquiry. It is nice to support projects that will do wonderful things over the course of the funding but rather frustrating to find that they simply cease when your funds are no longer available. From a funding perspective, it is reasonable to look for projects that have the potential to continue the work into the future. Working with a collaborative can offer excellent opportunities for incorporating aspects of the project across agencies/organizations. The following discussion will lead you into planning for the future of your program. Do not be surprised if, again, this process reshapes the project in its current form and leads you to emphasize certain aspects of the project over others.

Sustainability: Determining Income-Generating Potential

In reality, most human service programs have the potential to generate some income through the services they provide. However, as many clients are unable to pay the full cost of the services, future funding plans often combine the income that can be generated for services and materials with some combination of new grants and contracts. Ask yourself the following questions to ascertain if the project has the potential to generate some income on its own:

- Can you charge your clients a fee-for-service?
- Is it possible to market products or materials developed under the project?
- Can you ask your program recipients for a donation?
- How can a collaborative sustain the program through a fee structure?

The Life Cycle of a Project

What happens when you forecast the project over a five-year period? This perspective is useful for seeing as yet unrecognized potential for the project. Consider the project as having three stages:

1. The project relies totally upon public and private funds as you develop and implement it.
2. You receive some income as a result of implementing a fee-for-service structure, receiving some grant money, and benefiting from some donated services of both volunteers and product. You are also selling some of the products and materials developed by the project in the first one to two years.
3. By the end of the five years, the project has enough income to enable at least a small-scale program to continue.

Multisource Funding

Consider if perhaps there is a way to tie the service into other markets over the course of the funding so as to develop a future for the project. For example, the program you are delivering may also meet the needs of individuals in the workplace. You may develop contacts with corporations over the course of the contract that will maintain services in the future. In other words, you will charge the corporations full-fee for the services and use this income to subsidize low-income clients.

Some opportunity may exist to seek corporate advertising donations to support your project, especially if the company has an interest in reaching a particular target group. You might include a corporate sponsorship in a newsletter, on materials developed for community use, or on an agency home page. The steps you take to ensure the continuance of your project into the future will pay off significantly. You will want to write the answers to these questions with optimism for the future and creativity. In fact, what you plan for the future just may come true!

Institutionalization of the Project

It is extremely useful to consider ways to *institutionalize* your project, meaning to imbed it in existing service delivery systems such as schools, hospitals, or churches so that it continues when you have completed the contract. For example, say the state is funding drug prevention education programs for middle school students. Can you design the program so that it provides direct services and teacher training in Year 1, so that a minimum of supportive service and training is required in Year 2 when the funding ends? This approach will allow the program to continue into the future with minimal funding.

5

WRITING THE NEEDS
OR PROBLEM STATEMENT

Chapter topics:

o Definitions

o The purpose of the needs statement

o A guide to writing the needs statement

The *needs statement* or *problem statement* provides the rationale for the request for funding and uses data and other objective resources that substantiate the need for finding a solution to the concern. This chapter will guide you through the process for crafting a need/problem statement.

DEFINITIONS

The term *needs statement* is generally used in seeking funding for programs or services, while *problem statement* usually applies to social or community concerns or research-oriented proposals. Oftentimes, the terms are used interchangeably; for our purposes, we will use both terms in this chapter. Our primary focus is on proposals written to improve conditions or address a problem existing within your community.

As outlined in Chapter 4, you begin the proposal development process with an understanding of the need or problem as the basis for conceptualizing your proposed program or intervention. Likewise, when you begin writing the proposal, the needs/problem statement is typically the first section completed. It provides a convincing case regarding the extent and magnitude of the need or problem in your community, and it is written within the context of those who experience the problem directly or indirectly.

THE PURPOSE OF THE NEEDS/PROBLEM STATEMENT

The purpose of the needs/problem statement is to identify the compelling conditions, problems, or issues that are leading you to propose a plan of action. This section of your proposal does *not* describe your approach to address the need or problem; rather it provides a strong rationale for why support should be provided. The needs/problem statement is rooted in factual information. The conceptualization of your proposal is guided by an understanding of the needs or problems, not only at the level at which you provide services but also within the larger context of the community, state, or nation.

An effective needs/problem statement does four things:

1. Uses supportive evidence to describe clearly the nature and extent of the need/problem facing those you plan to serve.
2. Illuminates the factors contributing to the problem or the circumstances creating the need.
3. Identifies current gaps in services or programs.
4. Where applicable, provides a rationale for the transferability of "promising approaches" or "best practices" to the population you seek to serve.

The needs/problem statement makes clear what requires prompt attention before conditions worsen, provides an explanation as to why the problem or need exists, and identifies some of the strategies used in other settings that could potentially address the problem or need in your area. You must thoroughly understand the significance of the needs/problem section, as it provides the very underpinnings of the remainder of the proposal. As stated before, the needs section is not the place to propose your particular solution or project. Rather, it lays the foundation for your particular solution to emerge as one that is responsive to the need.

The needs/problem statement provides an understanding of the impact of the problem not only on those directly affected but also on others, including the community as a whole. A compelling case should be made as to what effect continued *nonintervention* may have on individuals, families, and the community at large. One way to make this case is to contrast the costs of prevention or timely intervention to the ongoing costs of not addressing the problem. In addition, there are emotional and psychological costs to consider related to quality of life issues for the program participants and for the community.

Ideally, the statement is comprehensive but not boring. Be judicious in your selection of data and use that which most pointedly tells the story of those you intend to serve. Through the use of data, you want to

- Demonstrate that you have a thorough understanding of the problem and those you seek to serve.
- Demonstrate that you are knowledgeable of the types of interventions that are successful in addressing this problem for your client base.
- Indicate that you are aware of barriers that may hamper the provision of service to this population.
- Demonstrate that yours is the same issue that the funder wants to address.
- Lay the groundwork to lead the funder to the conclusion that your approach is participant/client-centered and clearly one of the best possible choices to address this problem.

A GUIDE TO WRITING THE NEEDS/PROBLEM STATEMENT

Obviously, you cannot use all of the data you find. Scrutinize it carefully to make the best possible case for your proposal. At this point in the process, many grant writers face the mounds of data in front of them with increasing anxiety. The problem now becomes one of condensing and editing the data to make a powerful statement within a limited number of pages.

Drawing upon the conceptual framework presented in Chapter 4, this guide now helps you organize the information to begin writing and breaks the needs/problem statement into sections. This is only a template to help you organize and is not meant to be your final version of the document. The examples we are using are based on hypothetical data—in other words, the data we use are made up for illustrative purposes only.

Section One: The Nature and Extent of the Need/Problem

This section could be subtitled: "What is the need/problem, and who is experiencing it?" In this section, you will try to provide a clear picture of the incidence of the problem (e.g., the number of people per thousand in the population who experience the problem and the rates by ethnicity, gender, age, and educational level).

In this example, we begin with a factual opening sentence that states the topic and captures the attention of the reader. We begin to define the problem and give a percentage of the total population who experiences homelessness in the geographical area to be served:

> The majority of families are only one paycheck away from homelessness, and for [number of people] in [your local geographic area], this fact is all too real. The majority of homeless [defined as those without semipermanent or permanent shelter] in [your county] are single mothers with children, representing the fastest-growing segment of the homeless population. These circumstances lead to poor school attendance and childhood health problems.

The next step is to compare the local-level data to the state and national data. If the incidence of the problem is greater than the state or national rates, your job is easy, and your next sentence might sound like this:

> In fact, in [year] the homelessness rate in [your county] was _____, which exceeded the state rate of _____ and the national rate of _____ in the same year [source of data].

If your rate is lower than the state and national rates, study the data and see if your county has experienced a significant change in the rate. You may be able to say something like this:

> Although lower than the state and national rates of _____ and _____, respectively, [your county] has seen a significant increase in homelessness over the past 5 years and, without intervention, will meet and exceed national rates within the next 5 years [source of data].

If your rate is so low as to make your application noncompetitive, you may need to find some other distinctive reason as to why your community's problem is significant. For example, you may have higher crime rates as a result of homelessness or more health problems within the homeless population. Contrast the high incidence of the problem to the low incidence of homelessness to make a stronger case. In this next paragraph, we address the issues of ethnicity, education, and length of time of homelessness:

> In (your county), the rate of homelessness by ethnicity is ___ % White, ____ % Latino, _____ % African-American, and _____ % Asian. The rate for [ethnic group] is disproportionately higher than all others. The average educational level for homeless people is _____ years of schooling; however, it is possible

that individuals with college degrees are, at some point in time, homeless. The average length of time that individuals are homeless is _____ months.

You will notice that we have not made a highly emotional appeal to the funder but have already put a face on the client in the first paragraph. We feel that the funder, as well as the human service provider, is all too aware of the personal toll these problems bring. Overdramatizing the problem can work to your disadvantage.

In the above example, the data are effectively presented within the context of the community. When you place data in relationship to other data (e.g., state or national level) or other associated problems, you strengthen your request and increase the sense of urgency. (Note below how effective the word *only* is when using comparative data.) For example, compare the following two statements:

Fifty percent of the young people in the county do not graduate from high school.

Fifty percent of the young people in the county do not graduate from high school, while the dropout rate is only 10% in the state and 27% nationally.

Section Two: Factors Contributing to the Problem or Conditions

In this section of the proposal you will address the causes of the problem and the needs of the clients. These may stem from a variety of factors, such as

- A lack of skill, knowledge, or awareness
- Debilitating attitudes or harmful values
- Physical or mental challenges and limitations
- Dysfunctional or problem behavior
- Limited resources or access to services
- Institutional and systemic barriers including fragmented services
- Policies, practices, or laws that have negative consequences (either intended or unintended)

In this section, you want to account for each of the factors that cause the problem. The following paragraphs are a beginning to that end:

A variety of conditions may ultimately lead to homelessness. Of the homeless population, _____ % have severe and persistent mental illness, _____ % have experienced the loss of a job, _____ % have recently divorced, and _____ % are _____ [source of data, year].

The top reason for job loss in the past year was personal health problems, including depression, followed by poor work performance, a lack of job-related skills, absenteeism, and health problems with other family members. In most cases, homelessness does not happen all at once. The family utilizes all available resources to maintain housing and often have one to three months of financial struggle before ending up on the streets.

A discussion of barriers to addressing this problem likely will be included in this section as well. For example, the stigma associated with homelessness may be so great as to cause people to delay seeking assistance, or the clients themselves may have attitudes or beliefs that prevent them from benefiting from assistance.

Each of these causes of the problem as stated in the above example is significant to program planning with different and/or complementary approaches and can be further developed along socioeconomic and cultural lines, if need be. The second paragraph, which indicates that homelessness is a process, is laying some of the groundwork necessary to support our project—early intervention to help shore up individuals to prevent impending homelessness—but, of course, we won't say anything about this in this section.

Finally, we want to warn you about one of the most common mistakes we see in this section of the proposal, which is known as "circular reasoning" (Kiritz, 1980). Circular reasoning occurs when one argues that the problem is a lack of the service that one is proposing. For example, you may write in the needs statement: "The problem facing many teens is that they do not have access to a teen peer support group."

After writing this, you may proceed merrily on your way to proposing teen support groups as a solution to the problem. The above statement, however, has failed to identify the needs teens have that can be met through a peer support group (e.g., loneliness, isolation, depression, and so on) and, in fact, gives the idea that the absence of a teen support group is the problem! Consider the way in which the following example might better address the needs:

An adolescent spends an average of ___ hours per day in contact with other teens in school and after-school activities. Research indicates that teens obtain approximately ___% of their information on drugs, sexuality, and health-related topics from their peers [source of data, year]. From a developmental perspective, teens are moving away from parental and other adult authority and into the development of their own personal authority. In this process, teens begin to attach to and relate to their peers.

Section Three: Impact of the Need/Problem

In this section, you want to look at the impact the problem has on the client, the client's family, and the community at large and the benefits to be derived through intervention, treatment, or prevention of the problem. The following paragraphs begin this process:

> The problem of homelessness exacts a significant toll on the homeless person and family. Children who are homeless are often uprooted from their schools and their friends, suffer from poor nutrition, and lack even the most basic of preventive care services (e.g., immunizations). If one is a homeless adult, one has no address or phone number to use to obtain employment.
>
> Once an individual is homeless, the demands on community resources are great. The Government Accounting Office has estimated that it costs taxpayers approximately $35,000 per homeless family per year to provide for the family's basic needs. In a study by _____, it was shown that timely intervention targeted at a family in crisis costs approximately $15,000 per year, a savings of over half of the cost of delayed intervention. In addition to the significant financial savings, homeless children suffered less days lost from school and improved health outcomes.

As you might have guessed, we continue to lay the groundwork for our early intervention project in response to the problem of homelessness. We want to show that our proposed project is cost effective and reduces the negative consequences associated with homelessness. But we won't say *anything* about the proposed project in this section, either.

Section Four: Promising Approaches for Improved Results

In this section, you can discuss the theoretical perspectives that have proven useful in designing interventions and successful approaches used in other geographic areas, and more than likely, you will discuss the barriers to improving the problem.

> Several promising strategies have been developed to address the problem of homelessness. The first is the Homeless Project based in Seattle, Washington. This project targeted a subset of homeless, drug-abusing adults using the psychosocial rehabilitation approach, treatment incentives, and comprehensive services. The program helped over 67% of its participants kick the drug habit, and after a year, 87% of those were employed and paying for their own housing.
>
> Other projects have been extremely successful in helping individuals in crisis avoid homelessness altogether. One project, in Michigan, opened a

one-stop service center for struggling families. Through a combination of debt counseling, psychological services, educational remediation, job training, and health services, a full 90% of clients maintained their homes. In addition, this approach has the advantage of avoiding public resistance to a homeless shelter in the community.

In this section of the need/problem statement, you are referencing the particular theoretical and practical program components that will be effective in addressing the need/problem. For example, psychosocial rehabilitation is named as a theoretical orientation and service component. It would be useful to describe this approach briefly, giving the success rate, treatment advantages, and cost effectiveness. Discuss the pros and cons of particular strategies and consider the unique needs of your participants. If a collaborative approach is planned, identify the advantages of this strategy over a single organizational approach. The methods section of the proposal, which we'll discuss in Chapter 6, builds on the rationale provided in the need/problem statement.

6

WRITING GOALS, OBJECTIVES, AND THE IMPLEMENTATION PLAN

Chapter topics:

○ Goals and objectives

○ Implementation plan

Understanding the needs or problems in your community and the capacity to address them leads directly into the development of goals, objectives, and a plan of action. This chapter is divided into two sections: Section One will distinguish between goals and objectives and discuss two types of objectives; Section Two will provide guidelines for developing the implementation plan. Together, these two sections describe what is to be achieved and how it will be accomplished. The next chapter will describe evaluation methods for determining whether your objectives were achieved. Table 6.1 refines the conceptual framework discussed earlier to show the connections among the sections of the proposal and identify the questions each should answer.

SECTION ONE: GOALS AND OBJECTIVES

Program Goals

There is often confusion between the use of the terms *goals* and *objectives*, and many times they are used interchangeably. For our purposes, we are distinguishing between them. *Goals* respond to identified needs or

TABLE 6.1   Conceptual Framework for Writing Goals and Objectives

---

Determine the problem/need
> What are the problems/needs?
> What conditions or circumstances need to be addressed?
> Who experiences or is impacted by them?
> What factors contribute to their occurrence?

State the goal(s)
> What is the *ultimate* desired result for changing conditions or circumstances?
> What are the agreed-upon issues/needs to be addressed in the long run?

State the objectives
> What will be the *immediate* outcomes, results, or benefits?
> What changes are expected during a specified time period that will address the problems/needs?

Describe the implementation plan
> What activities or actions will be taken to lead to the desired results?
> What theory of practice will achieve the expected outcomes?

Develop a plan for measuring the expected outcomes
> What are the short- and long-term indicators that measure progress toward the outcomes?
> What data will be collected to determine the extent to which the outcomes were achieved?

---

problems and are statements of the ultimate mission or purpose of the program or collaborative. They represent an ideal or "hoped for" state of the desired change. They are often described as broad, idealistic, nonmeasurable statements of well-being. *Objectives*, on the other hand, represent the immediate desired and measurable outcomes or results that are essential for achieving the ultimate goals. They provide more tangible evidence that the desired state was achieved. The goal of a program may be "to eliminate child abuse" or "to prevent domestic violence." The objective may be "to improve family functioning by 25%" or "to decrease by 10% the cases of reported domestic violence in Grant City." Most proposals identify one to three goals. Other examples of goals are

- To initiate movement toward a pollution-free environment in the United States of America
- To increase the number of pregnant women in the state of New York who receive early prenatal care
- To reduce the number of birth defects in Grant County

As you see in these examples, goals are ambitious statements—they are the desired state of things. As such, they are not generally attainable over the short term, yet they help us to keep our focus and communicate the project clearly to others.

Goals are usually written indicating the geographic area in which the services are to be provided. To write the goals, return to the needs or problems you seek to address and state the major reasons for your work. The following two questions can assist you in developing goals:

1. What satisfactory condition will exist if we eliminate, prevent, or improve the situation?
2. What is the overall, long-term condition desired for our program recipients?

In some cases, the funders may provide the goals associated with the funding. For example, when applying for funding through federal or state sources, the goals are usually listed in the Request for Proposals, in which case it is advisable simply to restate those goals, adding the geographic area of service. If you are developing both goals and objectives, double check to be sure that the goals fit within legislative mandates or other funding missions.

Formulating Objectives

Outcome objectives are the *expected* results of the actions taken to attain the goal. They provide the promise of what will be achieved over the course of the funding period. Outcome objectives are specific, achievable, measurable statements about what will be accomplished within a certain time frame. It is also useful to think of objectives as the steps that you will take to reach the goal.

Typically, three to four objectives are derived from each goal and are defined more narrowly, since you are predicting that you will accomplish certain things within an agreed-upon time period. It is wise to develop objectives for each type of change expected and for each target group. For example, with the goal "To eliminate child abuse and neglect," several objectives may be targeted to parents, one to teachers, and a third to the community at large.

In collaboration, agencies can develop objectives that are either agency specific or shared among the agencies. Developing shared objectives within a collaborative can be especially challenging, since organizations must collectively take responsibility for the desired results. Shared objectives require a certain level of trust between agencies, since the objective must be met for reimbursement to occur.

Types of Objectives

The two major types of objectives, process and outcome, are explained below.

Process Objectives. Process objectives (a) describe the expected improvements in the operations or procedures, (b) quantify the expected change in the usage of services or methods, or (c) identify how much service will be received. Process objectives do not indicate the impact on the program recipients. Rather they are formulated because the activities involved in implementation are important to the overall understanding of how a problem or need gets addressed. They help to provide insight into experimental, unique, and innovative approaches or techniques used in a program. Process objectives are usually designed to increase knowledge about how to improve the delivery of services.

For example, process objectives might be written to measure different types and amounts of staff interaction with clients, to examine outreach activities with difficult-to-reach youth, or to describe interagency collaboration. A process objective focused on coalition building is not necessarily concerned with *what* is accomplished by the coalition but in *how* the coalition is formed and maintained. Process objectives may be written to study program implementation methodology, to determine whether the program is on track, or to address the internal functioning and structure of an organization, as in the following objectives:

- Ten child abuse prevention support groups will be formed by agency staff within the first 6 months of the project.
- A computerized client-charting system will be developed to track and retrieve 50% of client records by June 30, 20xx.

Both examples focus on the activities required to provide service, rather than the impact of those activities on the clients or participants. Process objectives are not routinely developed in proposals, since funders typically focus on giving funds for the direct benefit of the program recipients. In contrast to process objectives, outcome objectives are used to describe the expected benefits to program recipients.

Outcome Objectives. The second and more common type of objective is known as an outcome objective. An outcome objective specifies a target group and identifies what will happen to them as a result of the intervention or approach. Outcomes may depict a change at one or more levels, such as at the client, program, agency, systems, cross-systems, or community level (Gardner, 1999). Outcomes are usually written to indicate the effectiveness of the approach used by stating what will be different. Changes may occur in multiple areas such as

- Improved behavior
- Increased skills
- Changed attitudes, values, or beliefs
- Increased knowledge or awareness
- Improved conditions
- Elimination of institutional or systemic barriers
- More effective policies, practices, or laws

Well-stated *outcome* objectives provide the following:

- A time frame
- The target group
- The number of program recipients
- The expected measurable results or benefits
- The geographic location or service locale, which may be stated in the goal (e.g., group home, hospital, jail, neighborhood)

An objective may also identify the target group in terms of their age, gender, and ethnicity (if applicable). Objectives use action verbs (e.g., to reduce, increase, decrease, promote, or demonstrate) to indicate the expected direction of the change in knowledge, attitude, behavior, skills, or conditions. They define the topic area to be measured (e.g., self-esteem, nutrition, communication) and the date by which the results will be accomplished.

As you develop outcome objectives, think again about the needs of the program recipients and the community. Is the purpose of your program or collaborative to increase knowledge about certain topics so as to affect behavior? Do the intended program recipients have the knowledge yet persist in unhealthy behavior, leading you to work more directly on attitudes, values, or beliefs? What exactly do you hope to change? Will you focus on improving the conditions for a group? The objective should capture the primary purpose of the service you provide.

Many times, staff in therapeutic settings have difficulty in formulating measurable outcome objectives and are more apt to develop process objectives. Their difficulty lies in finding ways to conceptualize and make observable the progress of clients, especially those who are in non–behaviorally oriented counseling settings, and in subjecting the client to a formal evaluation process.

Thus, staff often find it easier to describe the therapeutic process as an objective, without stating a quantifiable or measurable outcome objective.

However, as funders focus greater attention upon results-based accountability and efficient allocation of resources through such mechanisms as purchase of service contracts, agencies will need to increase their capacity to measure their effectiveness and impact. Having an in-depth understanding of the nature of the need/problem and the factors associated with its occurrence, along with formulating a well-developed theory of change that identifies progressive indicators or benchmarks toward the desired change, can help guide the development of outcome objectives. Too often, outcomes are aimed at changing complex or chronic conditions within a short time period and are not rooted in a full understanding of what achieving those desired changes will actually take.

Furthermore, an organization's theory of change may not incorporate important factors that contribute to the occurrence of the problem. For example, the goal may be to reduce child abuse and neglect, while the outcome is to improve family functioning by increasing knowledge about effective parenting. At the same time, alcohol and drug abuse may be mediating factors against improved family functioning, which are not being addressed. Thus, "increasing knowledge" may be a necessary component in the theory of change, but it is not sufficient to achieve the stated outcome objective of improved family functioning.

One way organizations address this is to partner with other groups. Agencies can develop objectives that are agency-specific or that are shared with collaborative partners. Developing shared objectives within a collaborative can be especially challenging, because organizations must collectively take responsibility for the desired results. Shared objectives also require a certain level of trust between agencies, because reimbursement funding comes after the objectives have been met. A progression of outcomes is developed that identifies the change or benefits towards an overall desired end. The United Way of America (1996, p. 32) describes three levels of outcomes:

1. *Initial Outcomes:* the first benefits or changes that participants experience (e.g., changes in knowledge, attitudes, or skills). They are not the end in themselves and may not be especially meaningful in terms of the quality of participants' lives. They are necessary steps toward the desired end and, therefore, are important indicators of participants' progress toward it.
2. *Intermediate Outcomes:* they are often the changes in behavior that result from new knowledge, attitudes, or skills.

3. *Longer-Term Outcomes:* the ultimate outcomes a program desires to achieve for its participants. They represent meaningful changes for participants, often in their condition or status.

The following is an example of a short-term outcome objective focused on increased knowledge of the target group:

Two hundred pregnant women living in the Grant neighborhood will increase their knowledge by 40% about prenatal care by June 30, 20xx.

A longer-term outcome could be stated as

Eighty percent of the pregnant women living in the Grant neighborhood will access prenatal care in the first trimester by June 30, 20xx.

Sometimes so-called "proxy outcomes" are developed. For example, you may wish to improve birth outcomes by decreasing the incidence of low birth weight babies. However, this goal may be very difficult to measure. At the same time, research has shown a direct link between women receiving early prenatal care and improved birth outcomes. Therefore, one can use getting women into early prenatal care as a "proxy" measure for the desired outcome of improved birth weight.

The beginning grant writer is apt to confuse an objective with an implementation activity. A common error is to write the actual program or service that will be offered without indicating its benefits. Such an error would result in the following example of a *poor* objective:

One thousand youths between the ages of 12 and 16 will have participated in a 6-week education program on violence prevention by June 30, 20xx.

In this example, the "6-week education program" is an implementation activity and does not describe its impact on the participants regarding violence prevention. The following questions may help the writer to reach the outcome level of the objective: Why are youths receiving a 6-week program? To increase their knowledge or improve their skills? To change behavior? A revised, well-stated objective would look like this:

One thousand youths between the ages of 12 and 16 will increase their knowledge by 40% in conflict resolution and anger management by June 30, 20xx.

As you write your objectives, make sure you are stating the expected *outcome* or changes in the program recipients, not just identifying the approach being used. The following example shows how a single goal can lead to several process and outcome objectives:

Sample Goal: To prevent drug use among young people by promoting their academic success and emotional well-being.

Process Objectives:

1. To form a coalition of 10 youth-serving agencies to develop a comprehensive plan for providing after-school activities at two junior high schools by June 30, 20xx.
2. To establish a multilingual teen drug prevention hotline with a corps of 100 volunteer high school students by June 30, 20xx.
3. To develop a multimedia drug abuse prevention campaign targeted to junior high school students and their parents by June 30, 20xx.

Outcome Objectives:

1. One hundred at-risk junior high school students will increase their knowledge by 60% about the dangers of drug and alcohol use by June 30, 20xx.
2. One hundred and twenty five junior high school students who are academically at risk will show a 30% improvement in their reading and math scores by June 30, 20xx.
3. One hundred and fifty parents will increase their knowledge by 60% in effective communication techniques for teaching their children about decision making, goal setting, and the dangers of drugs by June 30, 20xx.
4. One hundred parents will increase their involvement with their children's school by 50% by June 30, 20xx.

In summary:

1. The *goal statement* provides a general aim and direction for the project, but lacks specificity as to what will be achieved.
2. *Process objectives* identify the approach to be used but do not state what impact it will have on the participants. It is not necessary for every proposal to have both process and outcome objectives. Process objectives are written when the funder has indicated that the desired outcome is to develop a new approach or test out a particular method of service delivery.
3. *Outcome objectives* specify "who" and "how many" are to achieve "what results."

Common errors in writing objectives include (a) putting more than one measurable outcome in the objective and (b) saying much more than is needed. Keep the objectives simple and clear. While you want to stretch as far as possible with a vision for improved conditions or circumstances, objectives should be realistic and not promise more than can be delivered within the time period stated. Remember also that objectives are directly tied to the contractual relationship between the agency and the funder, and as such, the agency may be held accountable if the objective is not met.

SECTION TWO: IMPLEMENTATION PLAN

Developing the Implementation Plan

The implementation plan is the nuts and bolts of the proposal; it provides a clear account of what you plan to do, who will do it, and in what time frame the activities will be accomplished. This section is the logical next step after writing the goals and objectives, for while the goals and objectives indicate *what* you wish to achieve, the implementation plan explains *how* the objectives will be achieved. It presents a reasonable and coherent action plan that justifies the resources requested. The design of your program should generate confidence that it reflects sound decision making and is the most feasible approach for addressing the need/problem. The program objectives serve as the foundation for developing the implementation plan and lead directly to the tasks and activities to be undertaken. A well-defined plan of action indicates to the funder the reasonableness and rationality for achieving the desired results.

This section will assist you in formulating a systematic and step-by-step implementation plan.

The discussion will be organized in three parts: defining the preparatory tasks, identifying the specific program-related activities, and writing the narrative.

Preparatory Activities

Regardless of the type of program you wish to undertake, a common set of activities usually are considered at the beginning of the project. We refer to these as "preparatory activities" (i.e., the start-up activities or general tasks necessary to get the program underway). With each task, it is also useful to identify the person responsible for accomplishing the activity and to estimate the time needed for completion. While the type of preparatory activities will vary, depending upon the nature of your program, the following, not listed in any time sequence, are typical:

- Developing staffing plans
- Selecting site/facilities
- Ordering special equipment
- Selecting or developing program products or materials
- Setting up interagency agreements and collaboration plans
- Building community linkages and partnerships
- Developing outreach strategies and approaches to involving program participants
- Setting up evaluation mechanisms

A variety of activities will need to be accomplished to achieve the program outcomes, most of which have resource implications. These resources include personnel (e.g., staff, volunteers, program recipients, community groups, other organizations), nonpersonnel (e.g., equipment, facilities, materials, and supplies), and other program-related costs. One must also be mindful of any restrictions or constraints on the program, such as policies and regulations that would affect how the resources can be utilized.

Program-Related Activities

In general, we have grouped human services programming into five major broad categories: (a) training or education; (b) information development and dissemination; (c) counseling, self-efficacy, and other support services; (d) provision of resources or changing conditions; and (e) advocacy and systems change. (There may be other subcategories, but we have chosen to address these major groups.) Remember that program design must be considerate of the diversity within the target population. While there is no single approach to developing the implementation plan, the following questions are designed to assist you in identifying the kinds of activities that might be required to conduct programs in the five major categories. You can use the answers from these questions to forge a coherent and workable plan of action.

Training or Education Programs

Examples: Career development workshop, job preparation training, parent education

1. What are the training or educational objectives?
2. What will be the content of the presentation(s)?

3. What strategies or techniques will be most effective with the population (e.g., teaching aids and tools)?
4. Who will conduct the training? What criteria will be used to select trainers?
5. What will be the typical format and schedule? Does it take into consideration the program participants' needs and schedules?
6. What other arrangements will be needed for the program participants to participate fully?

Information Development and Dissemination

Examples: Ad campaign for drug abuse prevention, videotape on AIDS prevention, health care newsletter, parent training manual, resource and referral service

1. Who is the targeted audience?
2. What will be the content and format?
3. How will it be developed? Who will develop it?
4. Which group(s) will review before distribution to determine effectiveness and appropriateness?
5. What dissemination strategies will be utilized?

Counseling, Self-Efficacy, and Other Support Services

Examples: Bereavement counseling, support group for victims of abuse and violence, drug and alcohol abuse counseling, and crisis hotline

1. What counseling strategies or techniques will be used?
2. What are the underlying assumptions or evidence of the validity of the techniques with the specific population?
3. What will be the counseling process and format?
4. What issues and content will be addressed?
5. What other resources (e.g., support system, professionals) will be needed by the program participants?
6. What are the plans to reduce the attrition rate?

Provision of Resources or Changing Conditions

Examples: Transportation for the disabled, meals program for older Americans, youth recreation program, health care screening

1. What resources will be provided?
2. What is the most effective delivery approach for the population?
3. When, where, and how will they be delivered?
4. Who will develop, organize, and deliver them?
5. Any special equipment and/or materials needed? How will these be obtained?

Advocacy and Systems Change

Examples: Legislation to ban smoking in public places, education reform, health care coverage for low-income families, alcohol and drug treatment on demand

1. What is the research and data on the issues?
2. What policies, regulations, or laws need to be changed?
3. What coalitions or partnerships are necessary to achieve the changes?
4. What are the most effective strategies to create effective change? What are important media strategies?
5. What compromises are acceptable?
6. Who will be the spokespersons?

Units of Service

In addition to identifying the tasks to be undertaken, one must also specify *how much* of that activity will be provided. This question relates to the volume of work that is expected or the products of your program, often referred to as the "output" of your program. It describes the types or amounts of service provided. Examples include

- One hundred hours of group counseling with 75 drug abuse addicts
- Two hundred health care newsletters printed and distributed to persons 55 years and older
- One hundred and fifty high school dropouts attending 10 hours of computer training sessions

The results or outcomes are influenced by how well the program has been conceptualized and whether there were sufficient units of service to achieve the objective. Compare these two examples of units of service in relation to the outcome of "remaining drug-free."

1. 75 drug addicts received 5 hours of group counseling
2. 75 drug addicts received 100 hours of group counseling

Both programs are providing group counseling, but they have different determinations as to how many hours are needed to achieve the outcome of remaining drug-free. In considering the units of service, one must often balance the resources available with a realistic understanding of how long achieving the desired change will take.

Writing the Project Narrative

This section may also be referred to in the proposal guidelines as the *project description*. It brings together your conceptualization of the work plan, including the preparatory and program-related activities. Included within this section are subsections sometimes referred to as the *scope of work*, the *methods section*, or *program approach*. Many times, grant writers are unclear as to how to proceed with the writing of this section, as proposal instructions may lack specific details about content and format. In our experience, if there are incomplete instructions, we then provide a complete explanation of the project, starting with the goal of the project, followed by the objective, the implementation activities, and a detailed description of the evaluation method. This section allows you to bring more detail into the narrative, including the rationale for your particular program and staffing levels, for example, than in any other section of the proposal. The following is an abbreviated example of a project narrative section:

> The Learning for Life Project has two goals. The first is to ensure that all children receive a quality education, and the second, to eliminate school dropouts. The first objective under Goal 1 states
>
> > *Objective 1.1:* Two hundred (200) low-income school age children in the XYZ School District will improve their grades one full level by June 30, 20xx.
>
> To accomplish this objective, each of the 200 children will have their educational needs assessed by a learning specialist and be matched with a tutor who has the necessary skills to help the child. In the first month of the project, the project directors and the learning specialist will select appropriate assessment instruments for the children. Relationships currently exist with the University of Grant State and Grant City College to develop the tutoring pool. Faculty in the School of Education at these universities will assess student abilities, and the tutors will be ready to be matched by the second month of the project. The tutors will spend approximately 100 hours a year with each of their students during the regular school day (see Appendix on "Estimating Time"). The evaluation of this objective will be accomplished by assessing student grade point averages at the start of tutoring, based on their grades of the previous quarter, and comparing them to the grades of the quarter ending after the completion of tutoring. If students demonstrate an improvement in their grades by one full level, the objective will be met. The project director will be responsible for overseeing the implementation of the evaluation component.
>
> > *Objective 1.2:* Two hundred (200) parents of children in tutoring will increase their time spent providing homework assistance by 10% by June 30, 20xx.

(The writer will continue to address the implementation activities and the evaluation for this objective.)

It is not unusual to complete other subsections of the narrative, including the scope of work forms, a time line, or some other visual representation of the project. Experienced grant writers appreciate the opportunity to present the project activities in a variety of formats to ensure that the reviewers have a complete understanding of how the objectives will be achieved. In addition, computer-generated charts, figures, and project flow diagrams (see Schaefer, 1985 & 1987) are often used to enhance the presentation.

Scope of Work

As stated above, many state agencies require a scope of work form, which provides the basis for the legal contract. This format is useful for conceptualizing the various parts of the project, for it shows the relationship among the goal, the objectives, the activities, and staff responsible for the activities; a time line; and the evaluation. This is somewhat redundant to the narrative, but it does offer the advantage of a quick, one-page synopsis of each objective, implementation activity (approach), time line, and evaluation. In Table 6.2, we have filled out a scope of work form using the above example.

As you study the scope of work form, you will notice that the goal is written across the top of the page and is numbered (for example, Goal #1). The first column contains an objective that is numbered in sequence relative to the goal to which it applies.

The second column identifies the major activities that will accomplish the particular objective. It is also customary to list underneath each activity the job title of the responsible individual(s).

The third column, the time line column, indicates the start and end date for each activity.

The final column is for the evaluation of the objective, which identifies how each objective will be measured to determine if it has been achieved.

Project Time Line

In addition to seeing a description of the project activities, funders typically desire to see a schedule of those activities. A visual display of the action plan provides the reader with a real sense of when different phases of the project will be undertaken. It also helps to generate confidence in your ability to plan effectively and carry out the grant or contract requirements.

TABLE 6.2   Scope of Work Form

Contractor *Geta Grant Agency*

Contract Number _____

Agency Number _____

Scope of Work

County *Grant County*

The contractor shall work toward achieving the following goals and will accomplish the following objectives. This shall be done by performing the specified activities and evaluating the results using the listed methods to focus on process and/or outcome.

Goal No. __I__ (specify) ___To ensure that all children receive a quality education___

Measurable Objective(s)	Implementation Activities	Time Line	Methods of Evaluating Process and/or Outcome of Objectives
1.1 Two hundred (200) school age children will improve their grades by 20% by June 30, 20xx	1.1.A. The educational needs of the students will be assessed. (Learning Specialist, Project Director)	7/1/xx to 11/30/xx	1.1.A. Student grade point averages will be obtained for the quarter prior to tutoring and the quarter following the end of tutoring. If a 20% increase in grades is accomplished, the objective will be met. (Project Director, Learning Specialist)
	1.1.B. Assessment instruments for the children will be reviewed and selected for use. (Learning Specialist)	7/1/xx to 8/31/xx	
	1.1.C. Students will be matched with tutors who will spend approximately 100 hours with each. (Project Director)	10/1/xx to 4/30/xx	
	1.1.D. Student grade point records will be obtained for appropriate quarters to conduct evaluation. (Project Director)	10/1/xx to 6/15/xx	

TABLE 6.3   GANTT Chart

Geta Grant Agency

Project "Learning for Life" Time Line

Fiscal Year 20xx to 20xx

Objective	Jul	Aug	S	O	N	D	Jan	Feb	Mar	Apr	May	Jun
Objective 1.1: 200 school-age children will improve their grades by 20% by June 30, 20xx												
Identify and select assessment protocols	X	X										
Assess students' learning needs		X	X	X	X							
Faculty assesses tutors' abilities		X	X									
Students and tutors matched			X	X								
Tutoring begins				X	X	X	X	X	X	X		
Pretutoring grades collected from school sites			X	X	X	X	X	X	X	X		
Posttutoring grades collected						X	X	X	X	X	X	X
Evaluation report						X			X			X
Objective 1.2: 200 parents of children in tutoring will increase their time spent providing homework assistance by 10% by June 30, 20xx												
Continue implementation activities												

A variety of techniques can be used to present the project's timetable. One of the most common is a GANTT chart, which shows activities in relation to a time dimension (see Table 6.3). In preparing a GANTT chart, perform the following steps:

1. List the major activities and tasks.
2. Estimate the amount of time to be expended on each activity or task.
3. Determine how the activity is spread across a time period.

The time period is typically divided into months or quarters, and an activity's begin and end points are depicted with row bars, Xs, or similar markings. Generally on a GANTT chart, activities are listed in the order in which they will be accomplished (a forward sequence).

By examining the GANTT chart, one sees which activities are to occur within a particular time frame, which can be useful for project monitoring. Also, some funders require quarterly reports, and from the GANTT chart, they can determine what you plan to accomplish each quarter. It is a good idea to include the preparation of any reports to the funder as an activity on the chart.

If there are few activities or the project has a relatively short time span, the time line format shown in Table 6.4 may be used.

TABLE 6.4   Time Line

Geta Grant Agency

Project "Learning for Life" Time Line

Fiscal Year 20xx to 20xx

Activity	*Time*
Hire staff	July 1 to July 30
Train staff	August 1 to September 15
Develop curriculum	July 1 to September 30
Schedule workshops	August 15 to September 30
Conduct workshops	October 1 to May 30
Conduct evaluation	October 1 to May 30
Prepare final report	June 1 to June 25

7

WRITING THE
EVALUATION PLAN

Chapter topics:

- The benefits of evaluation
- Developing an evaluation plan
- Writing the evaluation section
- Other evaluation considerations

The evaluation plan provides feedback on how well you accomplished the stated objectives and can direct you toward areas for continuous improvement. The focus of this chapter is to provide you with a general framework for conceptualizing the evaluation of your proposed program and for preparing this section of your proposal.

THE BENEFITS OF EVALUATION

There are many advantages of having a sound evaluation plan, for it is through the development of effective evaluation strategies that major strides have been made in human service programming. Gone are the days where it was simply sufficient to do "good." Now the need is urgent both to "prove" that good and necessary things are done (outcome evaluation) and to document how they were done (process evaluation). Moreover, the transferability of best practices is enhanced when evidence supports that, indeed, the approaches used are related to positive results.

Evaluation research can be used in making assessments about the merit of programs, techniques, and program materials. From a broad view, the results of such research can form the basis of position papers for lawmakers as well as the creation of advocacy groups for certain causes. Within the grant-making process, the benefits of evaluation research and data can be viewed from two perspectives: the funder's and the organization's.

Funder's Perspective

From the perspective of the funder, the results of your evaluation may be used to

1. Determine whether the funds were used appropriately and whether the objectives, as stated in the proposal, were accomplished.
2. Assess if the program's benefits are worth the cost.
3. Assist in the development of future funding objectives addressing the same needs/problems.
4. Promote positive public relations through advertising the benefits derived through their funded projects.

Organization's Perspective

From the perspective of the organization, evaluation has the following benefits:

1. Compels the organization to clarify program objectives so that they are measurable.
2. Helps the agency to refine continually its approaches to service.
3. Provides feedback on the level of effort and cost required to accomplish the tasks so that adjustments may be made in the future.
4. Increases the organization's capacity to meet the need through increased knowledge about those they serve and effective interventions.
5. Assists the organization to communicate the benefits of its services to the public, thereby increasing public support.
6. Assists other organizations in program development through the dissemination of results.

DEVELOPING AN EVALUATION PLAN

In most human service agencies, evaluation plans are kept fairly simple due to a number of factors, including financial concerns, constraints imposed by the program recipients, the environment of the program, and limited staff expertise in evaluation methodology. When the program is part of a collaborative effort, data collection and sharing may be especially challenging. Funders will sometimes provide guidelines on the evaluation design expected, or they may simply state that an assessment of the program's accomplishments is required. Read the Request for Proposal or application instructions carefully to ascertain the nature of the evaluation desired.

When you design an evaluation, remember that you are developing a plan to determine whether the stated objectives were achieved. The objectives represent the "promise," while the evaluation provides evidence that the promise was fulfilled. Different terms are associated with different types of evaluations: *impact, product, process, outcome, formative,* and *summative* evaluations are just a few. In this chapter, we will briefly describe the features of a process evaluation but focus more directly on developing a plan to measure your outcome results. Increasingly, staff are expected to provide extensive information about the direct benefits of the program to the participants (or the community). Much is being written about outcomes evaluation, results-based accountability, and impact studies. It is essential that time and resources be invested in embedding programs within a results-focused framework. A process evaluation and an outcomes evaluation answer different questions; when used in combination, they can provide a more complete picture of the manner in which the program was implemented and to what extent the outcomes were achieved.

Goals of a Process Evaluation

As stated in the previous chapter, a process evaluation provides an assessment of the procedures used in conducting the program. A primary goal of this type of evaluation is to gather feedback during the operation of the program to determine whether changes are warranted. The results can also be incorporated to improve the implementation of a subsequent program with a similar focus.

Process evaluation provides an understanding of how you achieved the results; that is, it describes what happened, how the activities were accomplished, and at what level of effort. Conducting this type of evaluation requires close monitoring of the program and may include

- Assessment of participant satisfaction with the program
- Detailed tracking of staff efforts
- Assessment of administrative and programmatic functions and activities
- Determining program efficiency

Such an assessment can provide information on the level of staff effort necessary to achieve certain program results, the level of outreach necessary to reach clients, and the level of participant satisfaction with the staff, facilities, and/or program.

For example, in addition to determining whether there was improvement in family functioning (outcome evaluation), you may also be interested in assessing the effectiveness of different family outreach methods used (process). To undertake this latter evaluation, you would identify the outreach activities that attracted families to your program (e.g., flyers, public speaking, newspaper articles, directory listings, referral through other agencies, and so on). You might then survey the families to determine which outreach strategies they responded to as well as measure the level of effort and cost involved with each strategy.

Process evaluation goals may focus on the delivery of a particular service or colocated services of a collaborative, or they may assess the entire operation. The following is a sample of the kinds of questions that may be associated with various program objectives. These can guide you in formulating a process evaluation.

Training or Education Programs

1. What is the content of the training? What are the unique features of the training?
2. How is the training conducted? What procedures, techniques, materials, and products are used? What is the background of the trainer(s)? What costs are associated with the training?
3. What are the backgrounds of the individuals trained? Which training techniques are most effective with which groups?
4. What are staff's perceptions of the quality of the training? How can it be improved? What level of effort is required to accomplish each facet of the training?

Products/Materials Development

1. What and how are the products/materials developed and tested?
2. How are the products/materials disseminated?
3. How are the products used, including how often, by whom, and by how many?
4. What are user and staff perceptions about the products/materials?
5. What are the cost savings associated with the products/materials?

Improving Operations or Procedures

1. What is the nature of the improved operations or procedures? How do they contrast with the previous ones?
2. What is the implementation process for the new procedures or operations?
3. How do the new procedures or operations affect service? Contrast cost savings and level of effort between old and new.

Improving Conditions

1. What was the theory of change, and what was the change process?
2. Which techniques/methods are most effective at improving the conditions?
3. How does the change process impact agency or collaborative operations, including staff roles?
4. What are the cost savings?

Goals of an Outcome Evaluation

An outcome evaluation determines how well the program achieved its objectives. In contrast to a process evaluation, which answers the question "How was the result achieved?", an outcome evaluation focuses on "What and/or how much was achieved? What changes occurred in program participants or community conditions?" Funders are apt to expect such answers, since they are seeking some explanation of what was accomplished with the resources provided. This type of evaluation is sometimes referred to as the "so what" of the program: So what happened? So what was accomplished? So what difference did it make?

An outcome evaluation can be basic, simply being able to state what changes occurred in the program participants that are attributable to the program activities. Or the design can be complex, comparing the effect of different strategies or techniques on participants. In either of these cases, you are interested in the *results* of the intervention on the recipients. Figure 7.1 illustrates the conceptual framework for developing a results-based evaluation plan.

Four Steps to Prepare the Evaluation Plan

We have identified four steps in preparing a results-focused evaluation plan. These will assist you in identifying the major components and activities when developing the proposal. Our discussion will intentionally be cursory; for a more in-depth discussion, consult our references.

Figure 7.1   Results-Based Evaluation Framework

1. State the expected outcomes or results.
2. Determine the type of evidence needed.
3. Develop a data collection plan.
4. Identify data analysis and reporting procedures.

Step 1: State the Expected Outcomes or Results. As we discussed, your understanding of the symptoms and the causes of the needs/problems lead to the development of overarching goals. These goals are translated into measurable outcome objectives that indicate the changes or benefits to the participants. Your implementation plan represents your theory about what will work and how it will work to achieve those changes. Having well-constructed and realistic outcome objectives that are tied to reasonable time expectations is key to building a sound evaluation plan. (Refer to the discussion of levels of outcomes in Chapter 6.)

Step 2: Determine the Type of Evidence Needed. The next step is to identify the evidence that indicates the achievement of the outcome objectives. Often referred to as *indicators*, these measures are used to observe or quantify the outcomes. You should use indicators that are appropriate for the level of outcomes being measured (i.e., short-term or initial, intermediate, or long-term outcomes). They must be unambiguous: terms such as "much improved" or "highly successful" may be part of your outcome objective, but they do not provide enough specificity for measurement. You must define the amount of improvement necessary in measurable terms. How will you know the participants have improved? By measuring if they have increased their knowledge, observing changes in behavior, administering a questionnaire?

Determining the appropriate method to measure results takes time and a thorough understanding of what changes your approach will yield. When working in partnership with other organizations, agreement on the best approaches for determining whether the results were achieved is especially important. Questions such as "How will we know it when we see it?" or "What are the developmental stages toward the ultimate change desired?" or "How can we tell if knowledge, attitudes, behavior, skills, or conditions have changed?" can stimulate your thinking towards developing realistic and specific indicators. In recent years, there have been compilations of

TABLE 7.1   Common Indicators

Healthy births
   Increased knowledge about prenatal care
   Lower rates of low-birth-weight babies
   Higher rates of prenatal care in the first trimester

Reduced substance abuse
   Increased knowledge about the dangers of alcohol and drug use
   Percentage of youth in grades 7–12 who consumed of less than five or more
      drinks of alcohol on a single occasion in the last 30 days

Improved parent functioning
   Improved scores on parenting skills pre- and posttest
   Increased time spent reading to children
   Employment of nonviolent techniques of disciplining

indicators typically used in human services programming. Table 7.1 provides examples of common indicators.

In these examples, you will note that more than one indicator may be used to measure an outcome. Additionally, you may be measuring one variable in the short-term (e.g., did the participants increase their knowledge about a subject?). But in the long run for the same group, you may be interested in looking at another variable (e.g., did they change behavior, or are there different conditions?). In Chapter 6, we referred to proxy measures, which may be used as good representations of an outcome that is hard to measure directly.

Step 3: Develop a Data Collection Plan. Once you know the specific, observable measures or the type of data you will use to indicate whether an outcome has been achieved, you must develop a plan for collecting that data. Be sure to consider cultural factors when developing your data collection strategies. Such factors as cultural response sets, interpretation of the meaning of words, and mistrust or suspicion of how data will be used can affect the reliability of your results. There are several components, as shown in Figure 7.2.

Figure 7.2   Data Collection Plan

When determining the data sources, consider the level of effort and cost involved. Some data may be readily accessible and in a form that you can easily use. In other cases, more effort is needed to retrieve the data. Sources for data include

- Agency records
- Progress reports
- Time allocation records
- Agendas and minutes of meetings
- Activity schedules, agency calendars
- Telephone call slips
- Visitor logs
- Written requests for service or product
- Audio or videotapes
- Questionnaires, interview notes, program participant survey forms
- Standardized tests
- Staff notes and documentation of role plays, observations
- Service recipient intake and exit interviews
- Community-wide demographic data

In addition to determining the type and source of the data, you must also consider appropriate procedures for collecting them. In some instances, it may be more efficient and less costly to select a subset or sample of the participants; refer to a basic statistics book for more detailed discussion on sample selection procedures. In considering the data collection procedures, one must determine

- Persons responsible for developing or selecting the data collection tools
- How the data will be collected
- Whether measurements will also be conducted on comparison/control group(s)
- Whether the measurements are culturally competent
- Procedures for assuring voluntary participation in the evaluation
- Safeguards for protecting client confidentiality
- Sampling plans, including type of sample and size (if applicable)

Another dimension to consider is the point in time that you will collect data. These data collection points should also be indicated on the project time line. When considering the timing of the measurements, think about the benefits of collecting data at the following points:

- Before the project—which establishes a baseline (pretest)
- During the project—which monitors progress and reveals interim outcomes

- After the project—when used with baseline data, can show change over time (posttest)
- Follow-up, postproject — determines the long-term benefits

Step 4: Identify Data Analysis and Reporting Procedures. Review the evaluation plan to determine how you will represent the data. Do you want to show frequencies, percentages, rates, comparisons, and so on? Will you compare the outcomes of different subgroups by socio-demographic characteristics (e.g., gender, age, ethnicity, income levels) and/or by the amount of exposure to the project? Which statistical techniques will be most conducive to answering the evaluation questions? Review your evaluation instruments to ensure that you have included all of the variables you may need and an appropriate method to obtain the data so you gain maximum benefit from the effort.

Evaluation data are usually presented to the funder on either a quarterly or semiannual basis and at the project's end. Unless the funder specifies the reporting requirements, you should decide how you will keep the funder apprised of the program's activities and accomplishments.

WRITING THE EVALUATION SECTION

The decisions made about the evaluation design must be incorporated into a coherent presentation. Similar to the project narrative, funders have different expectations and requirements for writing the evaluation plan. Some will desire an elaborate narrative description, while others will request a brief outline or scope-of-work format. We will discuss both formats.

Narrative Description

If no specific instructions have been given for preparing this section, the following is a typical format. The decisions made during the conceptualization of the evaluation are now evidenced within this framework.

Outline for an Evaluation Plan

    I. Identify the evaluation goals
   II. Describe the evaluation design
  III. Identify what will be measured

 IV. Describe the data collection plan
    A. The indicators or type of data
    B. Source of data
    C. Data-collection procedures
    D. Timetable
 V. Identify sampling plan (if applicable)
 VI. Discuss data analysis techniques
 VII. Address protection of human subjects and cultural relevance
 VIII. Explain staffing and management plans for the evaluation
 IX. Identify reporting procedures
 X. Show proposed budget

Scope of Work

In some instances, the funder will provide forms or require a brief outline of the evaluation plan. Completion of the scope-of-work form or some similar format may be the only requirement for describing the plans for measuring process and outcomes. This shorter representation generally entails listing the objectives, implementation activities, and the types of measurements of outcome/process for each objective.

OTHER EVALUATION CONSIDERATIONS

This chapter assists you in preparing an evaluation plan for the proposal to measure process and outcome objectives. Other considerations may not be addressed in the proposal but should be weighed when conducting an evaluation.

In examining what was accomplished (outcome) or how it was achieved (process), one might also need to evaluate the rationale or premise upon which the program was implemented. You may find that your initial understanding of the needs/problems, your perceptions of the needed solutions, your organization's capacity, and/or the community's response did not yield the expected result. Your evaluation may call into question the appropriateness of the program's objectives. The objectives may not fit within the community, cultural, or organizational context. Such analysis and feedback can help to strengthen subsequent planning and implementation. This can be especially challenging when working as part of a collaborative, for it is difficult to untangle the direct benefits as well as the lack of success of a single organization. Rather, the cumulative and interactive effect of the approaches is being measured. It is imperative that constant monitoring and shared feedback be provided as the program unfolds.

Unless specifically stated as an objective, an evaluation may exclude an assessment of the service delivery process and structure. Yet unintended benefits and/or impediments to assessing the service delivery system may result from project strategies and activities. For example, one dimension in identifying the needs/problems is to consider potential service barriers, such as availability, accessibility, awareness, acceptability, and appropriateness. Developing an evaluation plan that analyzes whether, and how, the project addressed these factors could reveal serendipitous benefits or unanticipated obstacles.

Reminders

Always be aware that the evaluation can uncover *indirect benefits* of the project. Such information can be useful in expanding the program and identifying the full benefits of the approach being used. It can also be useful when seeking additional funding support.

As is the case in other phases of the project, there may be constraints on the research design. In human services, many factors go into shaping the final plan, such as a participant's language skills, length of time with the individual, the benefit recipient's willingness to participate in the evaluation, or even the volunteers' willingness to administer the evaluation. The environment in which the service is provided will also impact your ability to evaluate it. For example, if you hold a large public meeting and hope to pass out questionnaires, you will find that most people will carry them home, whereas in a contained environment, such as a classroom, you will have better control on the return.

Another constraint on the evaluation is that it does consume a great deal of staff time in planning, administering, and evaluating the results; in other words, it costs money. Many times, evaluation is kept simple to keep overall costs down. Ethical considerations can shape the evaluation plan as well. Depending on the type of research you desire, you may need participants' consent, to deal with issues of confidentiality or anonymity, or parental consent, if asking questions of a minor. Again, it is important to keep individuals' interest foremost in your mind and respect their right to privacy as you design the evaluation. If you are concerned about possible ethical issues in your evaluation, check your library or a local university for research guidelines with human subjects before proceeding.

Most major universities have research departments. Often, nonprofit agencies can connect with individuals who have specific expertise in evaluation and solicit their involvement in the project. It is beneficial to involve evaluators in the design of the project and its objectives; however, agencies are cautioned that sometimes evaluators may unintentionally skew the intervention in favor of the evaluation instead of the services. The choice of an internal or external evaluator is often governed by the amount of funding available. In some cases, when funders have given grant awards to several projects of a similar nature, they may contract with a research consultant to provide evaluation assistance to all of their funded projects. If you do not have outside professional researcher assistance, be mindful of keeping the evaluation plan within the reach of the expertise of the staff.

The easier it is to implement and analyze the evaluation, the more likely you are to be successful. It is essential that you involve the staff in developing the evaluation plan. Also, feedback from other professionals in direct contact with similar types of participants may reveal variables that you had not considered. Evaluation can be very rewarding for the agency and, ultimately, for those you serve!

8

CREATING THE BUDGET

Chapter topics:

○ Types of budgets

○ Budgeting for the first-time grant writer

○ Other budget issues

This chapter is divided into three sections. The first differentiates three major types of budgets. The second is written for the first-time proposal writer and proceeds on a step-by-step basis through the preparation of a line-item budget. The final section discusses budget issues, including the preparation of a budget for foundation and corporate grants, budget adjustments and amendments, contract negotiations, and subcontracting considerations.

TYPES OF BUDGETS

The cost of running a program is expressed in a budget. As discussed in other chapters of this book, the program and the budget are closely tied to one another: a program costs money, and the budget tells how much it will cost and how the money is to be spent. For the most part, you need not be a financial wizard to develop a budget for a program. However, you will need to allow enough time to do the research to develop the budget wisely.

Budgeting for nonprofit organizations is becoming increasingly complex. Agencies are asked to respond to different funders' fiscal requirements and procedures, thus placing increased demands on agency accountants, bookkeepers, and administrators. The demands for accountability and

TABLE 8.1   Simplified Line-Item Budget

Geta Grant Agency

"Learning for Life" Project Budget

Project Term: July 1, 20xx to June 30, 20xx

Budget Category	FTE	Total Budget Request (in Dollars)
Personnel		
Project Director	1.0	56,000
Health Educator	1.0	38,000
Subtotal Salaries		94,000
Benefits @ 28%		26,320
Subtotal Personnel		120,320
Operating Expenses		
Rent @ $2/psf × 250 square feet		6,000
Supplies and Materials		10,250
Printing		7,390
Communications		4,800
Equipment		1,650
Subtotal Operating		30,090
Project Total		150,410

justification of resources are requiring different ways of viewing and categorizing funds. It is no longer sufficient for agency administrators to indicate what monies are being spent *on*; they are also being asked to describe what moneys are being spent *for*, that is for what purpose or result.

There are different types of budgets. *Line-item budgets*, discussed in detail in Section Two of this chapter, are most commonly required by funders. They represent the expenditures in specific budget categories (e.g., personnel and nonpersonnel). Two other budget types, *performance* or *functional* and *program budgets*, go beyond itemizing expenditures to providing information that can assist in the efficient management and allocation of financial resources. They help to provide useful feedback about the costs of project activities and program objectives.

A simplified version of a line-item budget is presented in Table 8.1. A total amount is developed for each budget line item, and all the lines are added together to create a project total.

TABLE 8.2   Functional Budget

Geta Grant Agency

Budget for the "Learning for Life" Project

Fiscal Year 20xx to 20xx

	Program Budget		
Functional Budget Activities	*Objective A: Parents*	*Objective B: Teens*	*Total*
1. Develop training curriculum			
Line items			
Personnel	$20,000	$14,820	$34,820
Rent	1,000	1,000	2,000
Supplies and materials	3,000	2,000	5,000
Printing	3,000	3,000	6,000
Communications	1,500	1,000	2,500
Equipment	550	450	1,000
Activity #1 subtotal	$29,050	$22,270	$51,320
2. Conduct training and groups			
Personnel	$45,000	$40,500	$85,500
Rent	2,000	2,000	4,000
Supplies and materials	2,500	2,750	5,250
Printing	450	940	1,390
Communications	1,300	1,000	2,300
Equipment	275	375	650
Activity #2 subtotal	$51,525	$47,565	$99,090
Total project	$80,575	$69,835	$150,410

A functional budget organizes expenditures according to a specific agency's program or by a project's objectives. From a properly constructed functional budget, one can determine the costs of performing certain units of work (Lauffer, 1997). Thus, one can ascertain the cost differentials between objectives. The functional budget example provided in Table 8.2 looks at the costs associated with achieving each objective of the program.

Some funders will provide an actual form on which to submit the budget request. The form provided in Table 8.3 is a copy of the federal budget form called "Standard Form 424A," and interestingly enough, it can be used to

TABLE 8.3 Federal Budget Standard Form 424A

80

BUDGET INFORMATION - Non-Construction Programs

SECTION A - BUDGET SUMMARY

Grant Program Function or Activity (a)	Catalog of Federal Domestic Assistance Number (b)	Estimated Unobligated Funds		New or Revised Budget		
		Federal (c)	Non-Federal (d)	Federal (e)	Non-Federal (f)	Total (g)
1.		$	$	$	$	$ 0.00
2.						0.00
3.						0.00
4.						0.00
5. Totals		$ 0.00	$ 0.00	$ 0.00	$ 0.00	$ 0.00

SECTION B - BUDGET CATEGORIES

6. Object Class Categories	GRANT PROGRAM, FUNCTION OR ACTIVITY				Total
	(1)	(2)	(3)	(4)	(5)
a. Personnel	$	$	$	$	$ 0.00
b. Fringe Benefits					0.00
c. Travel					0.00
d. Equipment					0.00
e. Supplies					0.00
f. Contractual					0.00
g. Construction					0.00
h. Other					0.00
i. Total Direct Charges (sum of 6a-6h)		0.00	0.00	0.00	0.00
j. Indirect Charges					0.00
k. TOTALS (sum of 6i and 6j)	$	$ 0.00	$ 0.00	$ 0.00	$ 0.00
7. Program Income	$	$	$	$	$ 0.00

SECTION C - NON-FEDERAL RESOURCES

(a) Grant Program	(b) Applicant	(c) State	(d) Other Sources	(e) TOTALS
8.	$	$	$	$ 0.00
9.				0.00
10.				0.00
11.				0.00
12. TOTAL (sum of lines 8-11)	$ 0.00	$ 0.00	$ 0.00	$ 0.00

SECTION D - FORECASTED CASH NEEDS

	Total for 1st Year	1st Quarter	2nd Quarter	3rd Quarter	4th Quarter
13. Federal	$ 0.00	$	$	$	$
14. Non-Federal	0.00				
15. TOTAL (sum of lines 13 and 14)	$ 0.00	$ 0.00	$ 0.00	$ 0.00	$ 0.00

SECTION E - BUDGET ESTIMATES OF FEDERAL FUNDS NEEDED FOR BALANCE OF THE PROJECT

(a) Grant Program	FUTURE FUNDING PERIODS (Years)			
	(b) First	(c) Second	(d) Third	(e) Fourth
16.	$	$	$	$
17.				
18.				
19.				
20. TOTAL (sum of lines 16-19)	$ 0.00	$ 0.00	$ 0.00	$ 0.00

SECTION F - OTHER BUDGET INFORMATION

21. Direct Charges:	22. Indirect Charges:

23. Remarks:

provide a program budget or a functional budget. The form comes with general instructions, and the RFA/RFP will include specific instructions for the type of project request you are submitting. Although you may be able to determine how to fill out this form, we recommend that, for your first encounter with it, you consult with someone who is familiar with it (an accountant or agency personnel perhaps).

BUDGETING FOR THE FIRST-TIME GRANT WRITER

The most common budget format for expressing expenditures in each category is a line-item budget, where each expenditure is itemized under its appropriate category. You are probably already familiar with a line-item budget for home budgeting with a line for each home expense such as food, rent, clothing, insurance, tuition, etc. In a proposal, budgets for a project are divided into two main categories: personnel costs and operating expenses. Personnel costs include the salaries and benefits of the staff required to do the project. Operating expenses include nonpersonnel expenditures such as rent, printing, mailing, travel, telephone, utilities, and office supplies. (Consultants to a project are sometimes included in "Personnel" and sometimes in "Operating Expenses." If in doubt as to where to place consultant compensation, consult the funder.)

The project on which you are working will probably be a piece of the entire agency service picture. It will represent a percentage of the agency's total program. If this is the case, the agency will establish a cost center (an account) to receive and expend the money for that particular project. The agency will also divide certain costs among the different programs it manages, usually according to the percentage that the project represents of total agency budget. A simple way to understand this is to consider the issue of paying the rent. If there are four sources of money through projects coming into the agency, all using equal amounts of office space, the agency could charge each fund 25% of the rent. If the proposal you are writing will be the only source of income to the agency, rent would be charged at 100%.

If you are working for a large agency, these accounting practices will be well established, and the accounting department can tell you exactly what it will cost the agency to run the program. Give the accountant or controller specific information regarding your program's use of the agency's resources. For example, estimate the number of copies you will make on the agency's copy machine during the project year, the number of pieces of mail you will send out, the cost of phone calls, and so on. In addition, if you are working for a large agency, you can rely upon in-house expertise in determining program costs, and you will have an already established salary range for employees. Plan to allow enough time for the accountant to respond and provide cost figures based on your projected use of resources.

If you are writing the budget for a new agency, or a very small agency, there may not be an accountant on whom you can depend. There may be no predetermined salary range for the personnel you propose to hire or no estimates of the costs of telephone or copier service. The job of writing the budget now becomes a bit more complex, and you must determine what this program will cost. The remainder of this chapter is be devoted to the grant writer who has little or no support to develop the budget. How does one begin? The following discussions will take you step-by-step through determining personnel costs.

Personnel Costs

Types of Staff Needed

What kind of staff do you need to run the project? Here are some examples of the type of staffing you might need:

Project Director: Will have overall administrative responsibility for the project and some direct service responsibilities. In most cases, funders will look for a full-time person in this role but may accept less than full-time if this is a smaller grant.

Professional Staff: Their education and expertise anchor the service delivery component of the program. These are the people who deliver the service. Perhaps they will be licensed therapists, credentialed educators, or health care providers.

Student Interns or Volunteers: Will deliver services that do not require a degree or special licensing or credentialing. This level of staffing often requires a training program to prepare them to deliver services as well as supervision (this training and supervision should be included in the program design and costs). Using interns or volunteers is a cost-effective manner to deliver services, and it contributes to the field as a whole as it builds the capacity of future professionals. Account for the resources that interns or volunteers will need to get the job done (e.g., office space, computers, Internet access, phone, mileage, and copying).

Secretarial/Administrative Assistance: Will manage phones, paperwork, scheduling, and other clerical duties.

Accounting Staff: Will manage the project's finances, pay bills and track expenditures, and prepare financial reports.

Executive Director: A percentage of this person's time or the time of other upper management will provide overall supervision to the project.

Time Required in Each Personnel Category

Now you want to determine the amount of time that the project will require of each staff position. This time is often measured in "full-time equivalents" (FTEs) and is expressed as a decimal. A 1.00 FTE represents the total amount of paid service that is the equivalent of one person working full-time for 12 months. To determine the decimal equivalent for a person working less than full-time, you divide the number of hours worked in a week by 40 hours. For example, if a person works 10 hours a week, dividing that number by 40 yields the decimal equivalent of 0.25. (There are 2,080 work hours a year in a full-time position.) In some cases, you may see a request for the "percent of time," which is expressed as a percentage. For example, if you are using percent of time and need a half-time employee, the position would be for 5O% time, or 0.50 FTEs. (See Appendix A for a discussion on estimating staff time.)

Determining Salaries

Determining salaries can be a difficult task. You may need to do some research into the local marketplace to see what people in comparable positions are earning. There are published reports on compensation in nonprofit agencies. For more help, contact your local nonprofit resource center or association. You may also get some sense of the appropriate salary range from the classified ads of the local newspaper or online job search sites. Once you have these data, consider any special skills that your position may require as well as what you think is "fair" reimbursement for the effort.

At this point, we also want to point out that the "poverty mentality" of social services is changing. In the past, social services paid notoriously little in return for the education and experience required to do the work. Most agencies have found that attracting and keeping top-quality people in the nonprofit arena is difficult. They have had to contend with a high attrition rate, which costs time, service, and money over the long run. Most funders today are well aware of the need to hire excellent staff to run a sound program and are willing to pay to do so.

An agency usually conducts a wage and salary assessment and establishes salary ranges for its employees. A salary range establishes the entry-level and top value of the position, say $3,000–$4,000 per month. Usually, "steps" within each range represent salary increases an individual may receive if they advance within the range. When you prepare a budget, you may be asked to include the salary range—but then which number do you choose to calculate into the proposal? If you are hiring a new person for the position, you may pay at the low to middle end of the range; but if you are using an existing, higher paid staff member, you may use the higher end of the range.

Personnel Budget Example

In the example in Table 8.4, you will see how each of the staff categories have been itemized, along with an indication of the FTEs, the fixed monthly full-time salary range, and the total requested amount for a one-year period. Note that the FTE has an asterisk by it, which refers to a footnote stating: "The FTE is subject to change during the contract year." This will provide some flexibility in the contract in case a vacancy occurs in the position or a need arises to deviate slightly from the stated time commitment. We have found this to be a part of some state contracts but not others, so just be aware that it exists.

As you see in Table 8.4, employee benefits are also included under personnel costs. It is up to the agency to determine what is included in this benefits line. At a minimum, this amount will include employer contributions for federal and state government-mandated payments (e.g., taxes, unemployment insurance, Social Security contributions); let's say this represents about 13% of total salaries. Employee benefits may also cover health and dental insurance and retirement funds, adding another 15% for salaries. The amount of benefit is calculated as a percentage of total salary, for example employee benefits at 28%. The total salary is multiplied by 28% to arrive at this number. Agencies set this percentage yearly as rates change, and rates may range from one agency to the next based on their specific costs. You will usually see a range from 25% to 35% but in some cases higher, depending on the industry.

TABLE 8.4   Personnel Budget

Personnel	FTE[a]	Salary Range (FTE per month; in dollars)	Yearly Total (in dollars)
Executive director	0.05	4,500–5,500	$3,000
Project director	1.00	3,000–4,000	42,000
Clerical	0.50	2,500–3,400	15,000
Subtotal salaries			60,000
Benefits @ 28%			16,800
Total personnel			$76,800

a. The FTE is subject to change during the contract year.

Operating Expenses

Now let us look at the second section of the budget, which addresses operating expenses. Again, it is important to look carefully at the proposal itself and identify all of the items that will cost money. The budget categories listed in Table 8.5 are typically found in project proposals.

Most funders will allow a certain percentage of the budget for indirect costs. It is acceptable to include costs for administration in this kind of line item under the operating expenses section of the proposal. Indirect costs are often included in a budget and cover such items as administrative costs, data management, IT management, unforeseen increases, audits, or additional expenses. There is usually a cap to the amount of this line in the range of 10%–15% of the total budget.

Many state and federal funders have established fixed reimbursement rates for such things as mileage, per diem, and consultants. Many will not allow for food costs in association with any training you may want to conduct. For the beginning grant writer, it may be helpful to contact the executive director of a similar type of agency for assistance with this category. Another option is to contact a local grantsmanship center or a university grants department and ask for the most current reimbursement rates in your state, or you can contact the state board of control that fixes the rates on a yearly basis. You might be asking, "Why don't I call the state or federal office to which I am applying for funds to get the information?" Because you will look like a beginner, and your position in the eyes of the funder may be weakened. Try to discover the answers to the above questions on your own first, and if that fails, then call the funder.

TABLE 8.5   Operating Expenses

Operating Expenses	Total
Rent (600 sq. ft. @ $1.30 per sq. ft. × 12 months)	$9,360
Office supplies	1,800
Printing	2,800
Equipment rental and maintenance	3,200
Telephone	2,400
Travel	2,580
Subtotal operating expenses	$22,140

Other details in the budget will not be apparent until you reach the negotiation stage. For example, you might have $5,000 in the budget to purchase a computer and printer. During the negotiations, if the funder tells you that they will not pay for the purchase of equipment but will allow you to rent it, you can then make the necessary adjustments. *Read* all of the instructions the funder gives on preparing the budget. Most funders state their restrictions in their application package.

Now we combine both the personnel and operating expenses into a typical budget format (Table 8.6) for project budget requests to the state.

TABLE 8.6 Typical Budget Format

Geta Grant Agency

Budget Request

July 1, 20xx to June 30, 20xx

Category	FTE[a]	Salary Range (per month; in dollars)	Total
Personnel			
Executive director	0.05	4,500–5,500	$3,000
Project director	1.00	3,000–4,000	42,000
Clerical	0.50	2,500–3,400	15,000
Subtotal salaries			$60,000
Benefits @ 28%			16,800
Total personnel			$76,800
Operating expenses			
Rent (600 sq. ft. @ $1.30 per sq. ft. × 12 months)			$9,360
Office supplies			1,800
Printing			2,800
Equipment rental and maintenance			3,200
Telephone			2,400
Travel			2,580
Subtotal operating expenses			$22,140
Total budget request			$98,940

a. The FTE is subject to change during the contract year.

Budget Justifications

In addition to a line-item budget, many funders want an even more detailed description of what is included on each line and how the totals per line were reached. In a budget justification, each of the lines is explained. The following is an example of a budget justification.

Budget Justification for Geta Grant Agency

Personnel

Executive Director: The executive director will be responsible for the supervision of staff, a small part of community networking, and overall program management, representing 0.05 FTE, for a total of $3,000.

Project Director will work full-time (100%) on this project with program implementation and evaluation responsibilities, staff and volunteer supervision, and report-writing duties. The salary is $42,000 per year.

Clerical: A clerk will be assigned 50% time on this project to prepare project correspondence, make phone calls to schedule programs, and respond to questions or requests for information at a total of $15,000. per year.

Employee benefits have been calculated at 28%, which includes FICA and federal withholding, SDI, state withholding, workers' compensation, and health and dental benefits. The total benefits cost for this project is $16,800.

Operating Expenses

Rent has been calculated at $1.30 per square foot times 600 square feet of space for a total of $780 per month. Multiplied by 12 months, that comes to $9,360 per year. Utilities are included.

Phone costs are calculated at $200/month times 12 months for a total of $2,400 per year.

Travel expenses include mileage to and from school sites and community meeting places: an estimated 335 miles per month at 43 cents per mile times 12 months totals approximately $1,730. Also included in travel is $850 for transportation and per diem (at State Board of Control rates) to one major conference for two staff members. The total request for travel is $2,580.

OTHER BUDGETING ISSUES

Some foundations and nonprofit trusts require a more simplified budget in which you indicate expense categories rather than itemizing line by line.

The budget in Table 8.7 places line-item categories into more general categories. This type of budget provides the agency with much more flexibility in the actual allocation of expenses, and the agency can usually transfer funds between lines without contacting the funder.

Matching Funds and In-Kind Budgets

When some of the costs of the project will be assumed by the agency, the agency is said to be contributing this money *in-kind*, and this portion of agency-borne expense is indicated in the budget. Some funding sources may require that the agency provide matching funds of a certain percentage of the amount requested. For example, one state office offered to fund 75% of the cost of providing a case management system to pregnant and parenting teens, with the applicant providing a 25% match.

One program director we interviewed called in-kind contributions "the creative writing section of the proposal." Examples of in-kind contributions are volunteer time dedicated to the project and donated goods or services or funds leveraged from another source, usually the agency's general fund, that are devoted to these services. The funds need to be focused on the services of this grant and, for the most part, cannot count as matching funds if they are paying for other services or if the clients who are receiving the

TABLE 8.7 Foundation or Corporate Budget

Geta Grant Agency

Budget Request

Personnel	
Salaries	$60,000
Benefits @ 28%	$16,800
Total personnel	$76,800
Operating expenses	
Overhead costs (rent, phone, utilities)	$14,960
Program expenses (supplies, videos, printing)	$4,600
Travel and conferences	$2,580
Subtotal operating	$22,140
Total budget request	$98,940

services will be reported to another funder. This practice is called *double counting* and is prohibited in most situations.

The example in Table 8.8 indicates one way to present an in-kind budget. The first column indicates the funder's portion of the total request, the second column indicates the agency's portion, and the third column indicates

TABLE 8.8   In-Kind Budget

Geta Grant Agency

Budget Request

July 1, 20xx to June 30, 20xx

Category	FTE[a]	Salary Range (per month, in dollars)	Funding Request	Agency In-Kind	Total
Personnel					
Executive director	0.05	4,500–5,500	2,000	1,000	3,000
Project director	1.00	3,000–4,000	38,000	4,000	42,000
Clerical	0.50	2,500–3,400	15,000	0	15,000
Accounting	0.10	3,100–4,200	0	4,800	4,800
Subtotal salaries			55,000	9,800	64,800
Benefits @ 28%			15,400	2,744	18,144
Total personnel			70,400	12,544	82,944
Operating expenses					
Rent			4,000	5,360	9,360
Office supplies			1,500	300	1,800
Printing			2,200	600	2,800
Equipment rental and maintenance			2,800	400	3,200
Telephone			2,000	400	2,400
Travel			2,000	580	2,580
Subtotal operating expenses			14,500	7,640	22,140
Total budget request			84,900	20,184	105,084

a. The FTE is subject to change during the contract year.

the total to be allocated for each item. Note that a similar format can be used if you are writing a proposal in which the resources are coming from more than one funder; indicate the source of the funding in each column, followed by a total funding column.

Budget Adjustments

In the line-item budget, the agency is accounting for expenses on a per-line basis. Most funders with line-item budgets do not allow the agency to transfer funds between lines without their consent. This process of requesting a transfer between lines is called a *budget adjustment*.

Table 8.9 shows an example of how a budget adjustment is presented. One column lists the current contract totals for the year, another indicates the amount of money you want to add or subtract from the column, and the final column indicates the new totals. With budget adjustments, you are not

TABLE 8.9   Budget Adjustment

Category	Prior Approved Amount ($)	Adjustment Effective 10/1/20xx	New Approved Amount ($)
Personnel			
Executive Director	$2,000	(100)	$1,900
Project Director	38,000	0	38,000
Clerical	12,522	0	12,522
Benefits	10,504	(20)	10,484
Total Personnel	$52,522	(120)	$52,502
Operating Expenses			
Rent	$4,000	0	$4,000
Office supplies	1,500	500	2,000
Printing	2,200	(380)	1,820
Equipment rental/maintenance	2,800	(500)	2,300
Telephone	2,000	0	2,000
Travel	2,000	500	2,500
Subtotal Operating	14,500	120	14,500
Total Budget	$77,526	0	$77,526

changing the total amount that you have to work with, just reallocating the money between lines.

The adjusted budget will most often need to have a written explanation attached describing what has happened, on a per-line basis, to necessitate the request for a change. In the explanation, you will tell the funder why excess money is in some lines while others show a deficit. The funder will be looking for a legitimate rationale to move funds between lines.

Budget Amendments

If during the course of the contract, your scope of work has been expanded or reduced, you may need to do a budget amendment reflecting this change. Here's a simple way to think about this. When you need to shift money and it does not alter the scope of work in any way, you write an adjustment. If something has happened to significantly alter the scope—for example, the funder has asked you to take on an additional project or activity and will provide more money—you will write an amendment. Some funders require an amendment if you are seeking to move more than $5,000 (or some other predetermined amount). Amendments are usually written using the same budget format as for requesting adjustments.

The major difference between an amendment and an adjustment is that the amendment changes your contract with the funder and goes through a formal approval process. You will receive a new copy of the contract with the amended budget and any program changes resulting from the amendment.

Contract Negotiations

When you negotiate a contract with a funder, be highly conscious of the possible domino effect that one change in a program will have on the entire program and the impact it will have on the budget. Most of the time, projects are designed so that the parts are interrelated and interconnected. Changing what appears to be one aspect of the project can have considerable effect on the whole.

Upon approving the proposal, some funders conduct formal contract negotiations. The negotiation is when you meet face-to-face, review what will be provided by the contract, and discuss a rationale for the implementation activities, the objectives, or perhaps even the goals. The funder may want to change an objective, increase the numbers, add a new objective, or clarify certain language. Most often, the funder approves the proposal for less money than you requested. For example, your request may have been for $175,000, but the funder allocates only $160,000.

A little caveat to first-time grant writers: you will be very excited that you have been funded. So excited, in fact, that you may be willing to do anything just to get the money and get the project started. *Be careful!* You can damage your project in the negotiations. The funder has a commitment to fund the project and will want the most for their money. No one knows the project better than you. Approach the negotiations from the perspective of win-win. The funder wants a good program just as you do. Here are a few guidelines for negotiating contracts:

- Re-read the proposal just prior to going into the negotiations. Be intimately familiar with all of it, just as you were when writing it 6 months ago.
- Create an atmosphere of partnership with the contract negotiator.
- Take your time when you make changes. Look at the impact any change will have on the objectives.
- Be prepared to discuss your rationale for keeping the project as initially developed in the proposal.
- If the agency has not been awarded the full amount requested, prepare a new version of the proposal in advance of the meeting. This gives you time to rethink the budget and program and decide upon revisions.
- Remember to maintain your integrity. If you know that the agency cannot do the job for the amount of money offered, despite changes to make the project more cost effective, the agency will need to decide if it is worth pursuing. It is possible, and we have seen it happen, that the agency will choose to turn down the contract because accepting it would be too costly.

Subcontracting

Subcontracting means contracting with another agency to provide a portion of the service in the proposal. Your agency receives the contract, and under that contract, you also have a contractual arrangement with another agency to deliver a service. Collaboratives typically use this arrangement. The subcontracting agency is bound by the same contractual terms as the primary contractor. The primary contractor is responsible for ensuring that the subcontracting agency abides by the terms of the contract and usually prepares a legally binding agreement with the subcontractor.

If you are utilizing subcontractors, you have to address this issue within the body of the grant itself to clearly identify, by objectives, the role of the subcontractor in the contract and to establish the credibility of the subcontractor in the applicant capability section. The budget of the subcontractor is included in the main budget and fully described in the budget justification.

As you review the steps in budget preparation, you can see why this should not be left to the last minute. Preparing the budget requires that you have a thorough grasp of the project, including all of the details of the implementation activities, so that you can be certain not to omit any major costs. Remember: Changes in the program will have an impact on the budget and vice versa.

9

AGENCY CAPABILITY
AND FINISHING TOUCHES

Chapter topics:

- ○ The agency capability statement
- ○ Requesting letters of support
- ○ The proposal abstract
- ○ The title and title page
- ○ The cover letter
- ○ FAQs

This chapter provides an overview of what some refer to as the "finishing touches" of the proposal. These are the items that complete the proposal and, except for the letters of support, are often prepared after the other sections have been written. Follow the funder's guidelines regarding the proper placement of these items in the proposal as well as how to bind the proposal. Most funders will provide a checklist for you to use in assembling the proposal and will indicate if they want a table of contents and/or separate appendixes.

THE AGENCY CAPABILITY STATEMENT

The agency capability statement establishes an organization's credibility in terms of successfully undertaking the project. It indicates who is applying for the grant, what qualifies an agency to conduct the project, and what resources (e.g., organizational, community) are available to support the effort. This section helps to generate confidence that the agency is programmatically competent and qualified to address the needs/problems and is fiscally sound and responsible.

In developing this section, the grant writer must reflect the agency's image of itself as well as the constituency's image of it. This includes describing the organization's unique contributions to those it serves and capturing the community's regard for these contributions. When preparing this section, one should provide quantitative evidence of the agency's accomplishments. A recurring weakness in capability statements is that agencies make qualitative assessments of the organization without supporting the claims with some corroborating data.

A capability statement should accomplish two things:

1. It should describe the agency's characteristics and its track record.
2. It should demonstrate how those qualities make it qualified to undertake the proposed project.

Many times, grant writers accomplish the first task but leave it up to the reviewers to infer the latter. They often fail to present a cogent argument that connects what they have done with what they are proposing to do.

When writing this section, avoid overusing the words *we* and *our*. It is appropriate to refer to the name of the agency or simply say "the agency" throughout the text. Write as if you are developing a public relations article for a national newsletter, informing the reader and making it interesting but brief.

When you are serving as a lead agency for a collaborative effort, you will highlight your agency's experience and also include subsections for each of the other agencies involved. It is customary to ask the participating agency to write its own capability sections to include in the proposal. A typical agency capability statement will reflect much of the following information:

- *Mission of the Agency:* the overall philosophy and aims of the organization.
- *History of the Agency:* a brief overview of when, why, and how the agency started and whether its focus has changed over time.
- *Organizational Resources:* a description of the agency's funding track record and of the human and material resources available to this project. (Include the pertinent background of staff, especially expertise in areas related to the needs/problems; other professionals associated with the agency; and any special equipment, materials, and services that can support the proposed project.)
- *Community Recognition and Support:* an indication of how the agency is regarded, including awards, accreditations, and honors bestowed upon it and the

staff, as well as how the community is involved in the agency's operation and structure (e.g., through membership, in programs, on committees, and boards).

- *Interagency Collaboration and Linkages:* a depiction of the linkages and support available from other organizations that can assist with the proposed project, including memberships in local, state, and national networks.
- *Agency Programs:* an overview of the unique programmatic contributions the agency makes to its clients and the community, including the aims and types of programs, and a quantitative picture of what is accomplished (e.g., the numbers served, the distribution rate of materials, the cost savings resulting from these services, and program outcomes).
- *Agency Strengths:* a description of the organizational characteristics that make the agency particularly suited to implement the project. In general, you indicate what is being proposed and how that fits with what the organization already has accomplished. For example, the agency may already be serving the target group, addressing the needs/problems, or using a particular technique or strategy that it now wishes to modify or implement in a different manner.

Supportive Documentation

Depending upon the funder, you may be expected to provide documentation on the agency's capability. These materials are usually placed in an appendix to the application. Be selective in the type of documentation you incorporate into the proposal. Typical examples include

- Letters of cooperation from other organizations
- Letters from other agencies or professionals attesting to the merits of the agency and the proposed project
- Letters from the agency's constituency, such as from clients, indicating the importance of this project to themselves and others in similar situations
- A copy of documents demonstrating agency accomplishments, including awards and recognition from local, state, and national groups
- A listing of the members of the agency's board of directors and their qualifications and affiliations
- IRS 501(c)3 letter
- Most recent audited financial statements

REQUESTING LETTERS OF SUPPORT

Most agencies phone a contact person in another agency, talk to that person about the project, ascertain the contact's willingness to write a letter of support, and then fax a letter specifically requesting support for the particular project. Typically in this letter, you would provide a brief synopsis of the proposed program, the funding source you are applying to, and specific instructions for writing the letter, including to whom the letter should be addressed and whether to mail it to your agency or the funder. We've included a sample of a request for a letter of support to other organizations.

Sample Letter of Support

The Geta Grant agency is applying for funding to the Office of Health and Human Services. In this proposal, we seek support for a case management system for Latino parents offered through the Families First Collaborative. Agencies included in this collaborative proposal include the Department of Education, A Fine Health Center, the Mental Health Center, the Human Interaction Commission, Housing First, and the Food Bank Distribution Center.

This project, called "Management for Health," provides a full-time case worker to address the mental health, educational, parenting, employment, housing, food, and health needs of the highest-risk Latino and White families in the cities of Lemon, Tangerine, and Banana. We expect that more than 100 families with multiple needs will be served in the first year. In addition, our project will evaluate the effectiveness of case management with this population.

If you see the need for these services in our community, and/or if you are willing to partner with us in this proposal to provide X, Y, and Z, please write a letter of support addressed to Mary Smith, Program Officer, Office of Health and Human Services, Department 007, 200 State Lane, Room 123, Our Town, California 90009; but send the letter to me: Grant writer, Geta Grant Agency, 1111 One Street, This Town, California 90002. We thank you for your support. Please call us to pick up the letter by Friday, June 2, 20xx.

As the grant writer, be prepared to make follow-up phone calls to the agencies and to pick up the letter if you are nearing the proposal deadline. It is wise to request the letters early, as you are preparing the other sections of the proposal, to avoid any delay as the proposal deadline approaches. In some instances, you may be asked by the organizations to draft a letter of support for them. This is often ideal, as you can be very specific about the items you want emphasized by each supporting source.

THE PROPOSAL ABSTRACT

The abstract is usually written after the other sections, since it gives an overview of the entire project. Unless the funder provides other instructions or forms, the abstract is typically no longer than one page. The abstract is used by the funder to screen the proposal for appropriateness in light of its funding objectives. A glance at the abstract also assists staff in disseminating the document to the proper review committees or funding offices. Once a proposal is funded, the abstract is often used by funders to convey to the public their funding decisions and activities.

Although it is sometimes hurriedly written at the end, care and attention should be given to its content. This is not the proposal introduction, but rather a summary of the entire project. As such, the abstract should parallel the major sections of the proposal. An abstract will typically

1. Identify the agency requesting the funds.
2. Describe the target population.
3. Summarize the needs/problems statement, highlighting data that show the magnitude or extent of the problem.
4. Provide a synopsis of the project objectives, including goals and objectives.
5. Highlight the evaluation plan and the expected outcomes or results of the project.
6. Provide an amount-requested figure.

THE TITLE AND TITLE PAGE

Develop a title that reflects the major goal(s) of the project. While a title may be catchy, its meaning should be readily understood by the reviewers. A descriptive subtitle might be used to clarify. Avoid long titles or titles that are used too often by other projects.

A title page usually accompanies the proposal. Federal and state agencies will often provide the face sheets necessary. While there is no standard format for the title page, the following is typical:

- Project title
- Name of the agency submitting grant
- Agency address
- Name of prospective funder
- Project begin and end dates
- Amount requested

THE COVER LETTER

A letter of transmittal on agency stationery, signed by the appropriate organizational official, should be prepared. The letter conveys interest in the funder's mandate and mission and states how the project fits within these mandates. The letter should be brief (usually one page). It should indicate the agency board's approval of the proposal, the contact person with telephone number, the amount requested, and the willingness to respond to any questions about the project. Include a paragraph that summarizes the project as well.

Remember that the letter is often the first contact between the agency requesting funds and the prospective funder. Set a tone of professionalism and competency. The letter should be written on agency letterhead.

A Sample Cover Letter

Dear Funding Officer:

Geta Grant, serving as lead agency for this project, enthusiastically submits this proposal, "Management for Health," in response to your RFP entitled "Community Funding Initiatives." This exciting collaborative partnership will provide direct case management linkage to a range of vital health services for the Latino community: housing, food, employment, mental health, physical health, and parenting. For the first time in county history, Latino parents will have an advocate and mentor to guide them through a system of services and allow them to deal holistically with their problems.

The partners in this collaborative include the Department of Education, A Fine Health Center, the Mental Health Center, the Human Interaction Commission, Housing First, and the Food Bank Distribution Center. As you will see in the proposal, each of the partners brings a wealth of services and expertise to our target population.

We are available to respond to any questions you may have about this proposal, and I may be contacted at (888) 888-8888.

Sincerely,
Project Director or Other Administrator of the Agency

You will want to present the funder with the final package in the format requested. If the funder asks for a certain number of copies or for the proposal to be bound in a certain manner (e.g., stapled in the upper left corner), you should comply with the guidelines. Be certain to leave enough time to review the final package after it has been copied and collated—this is a tedious task and requires attention to detail so pages do not get out of order. Once your packet is complete, send it on its way (signature required) to bring resources to those you serve in the community. We wish you many successful grants!

If the funder does not give you a checklist, the following may be useful:

____ Cover letter

____ Project abstract (sometimes included in cover letter)

____ Table of contents

____ Proposal narrative and scope of work

____ Program evaluation

____ Proposal budget and budget justification

____ Letters of support

____ Appendixes (e.g., agency financial documents, IRS determination letter, board of directors roster)

FREQUENTLY ASKED QUESTIONS (FAQS)

Q: What do I do if, after sending the proposal, I realize that I forgot to include an important section?

A. If you are still within the time line for submission, redo the entire packet and ask the funder to replace the initial packet with the new one. If outside of the submission time frame, e-mail the funder and ask if they will receive it from you. It can't hurt now.

Q: If we get turned down, is it okay to ask why?

A: Yes. Most funders will share the scoring process with you, and some may tell you how you can be more competitive in the future.

Q: I know a person who will be on the team to review our proposal. Can I submit the proposal in advance to this person?

A: This would not be considered appropriate, as it would appear that you are trying to influence this individual unduly to select your proposal. In most cases, readers are asked if they have a relationship with the agencies who have submitted proposals and are asked to withdraw from reading your particular proposal so as to avoid the appearance of favoritism.

Q: The funder has asked that I number the pages of the proposal. Do they want numbering on the pages in the appendixes as well?

A: Yes. Number everything starting with page one of the narrative. (Don't number the cover letter or table of contents pages.)

Q: How do I bind the proposal if the funder says not to use staples or notebooks?

A: Use a big paper clip or rubber band.

Q: It seems as though the funder keeps asking me the same thing. Can't I just reference my answer in a previous section?

A: We know how you feel—this is a common problem. However, you must keep answering again and again as many times as it takes. Don't reference a previous section.

APPENDIX A

Estimating Time

In this section, we provide an illustration of how to calculate a staff person's time expenditure on a project. Let's suppose that Geta Clinic wants to provide an AIDS prevention education program in the county schools. The objective states:

> Three thousand (3,000) at-risk youth will increase their knowledge by 30% on HIV transmission and risk-reduction behaviors by June 30, 20xx.

The implementation activities, with staff responsibilities, include

1. Relationship established with schools (Project Director, Community Educator)
2. Education programs developed and scheduled (Community Educator, Administrative Assistant)
3. Parent orientation nights planned and conducted (Community Educator)
4. Two one-hour educational presentations provided in the student's regular classroom on the nature of HIV transmission, risky behaviors, decision-making skills, and assertiveness training (Community Educator)
5. Student evaluation using pre- and posttests to indicate knowledge change (Community Educator and Administrative Assistant)

Someone without any knowledge about community education might say

Okay, this is simple. An average class size would be 25. Divide 3,000 by 25 to find out how many actual classes you need: 120 classes. Because the educator will spend 2 hours in each class, 2 hours multiplied by 120 classes gives a total of 240 teaching hours. If I divide 240 hours by 8 hours a day, then I need a community educator for 30 days.

The above reasoning process is faulty for a number of reasons. What factors need to be considered when implementing a community education program for Geta Clinic? The following discussion will provide an example of the kind of "thinking through" process needed to develop a more realistic estimate.

Access to the Community

Has the clinic ever provided educational programs in the schools? How much time will it take to develop the necessary relationships with the schools to gain access? How much time will be spent scheduling programs? How much time in community relations to develop the network? Will the sensitive nature of the topic impact this development time by making it even more difficult to gain access to the classroom?

Service Preparation, Evaluation, and Documentation

How much preparation will be required to provide the educational program in addition to direct teaching time? Will the educator need to write the curriculum? Will that person also need to evaluate the program's effectiveness? Grade the evaluation exams? Maintain other program records? Develop handouts for classroom use?

Geographic Location

How many sites can be reached in a day? Consider traffic patterns, distance, and climate.

Ethnic, Cultural, and Linguistic Considerations

Will the clinic need educators from different ethnic backgrounds? What languages will need to be spoken? Written? Is special knowledge required to work with this specific population(s), and if so, how much time will the educator need to acquire that?

Human Capability

Finally, consider what is humanly possible to require of a community educator in terms of actual teaching within a given day or week. The energy required in the classroom when the speaker is an "outsider" is considerably greater than when the audience is familiar with the person. Once the program has gained access to the schools, perhaps one two-hour presentation per day is all you can reasonably expect someone to do without burning out. Now let's recalculate the amount of time required from the educational staff. A full-time employee works 2,080 hours per year. You determine that the educator will need to spend time developing relationships with the schools. You might estimate that approximately 8 hours of contact time on the phone and in-person per target school will be needed. There are 50 high schools; therefore, to contact each high school would entail about *400 hours.*

Then you calculate that the educator will need approximately two to three weeks full-time to review the available materials and plan the curriculum. If portions of the curriculum need to be written and/or evaluation tools developed, those tasks would take, you estimate, about one month or *174 hours.*

We already know that the teacher will spend 240 hours in the classroom facilitating 120 different classes. Let's say you estimate that travel time will be 30 minutes each way, so that is 1 hour per class or another 120 hours in traveling time. So the time spent in classroom presentations and travel time totals *360 hours.*

You also calculate that the educator will need approximately 1 hour per class to handle the evaluation component, which comes to another 120 hours. You want a minimum of 10 hours per month available for improving skills and knowledge, updating records, attending an in-service, responding to correspondence, all adding up to another 120 hours for a total of *240 hours.*

Finally, let's add the fact that, due to the sensitive nature of the materials to be addressed, the Community Educator will need to make a presentation at "Parent's Night" so that parents can review the materials and ask questions. These presentations will require 2 hours at 50 schools for another 100 hours plus the one-hour travel time of 50 hours. The educator will also be networking with other community groups and getting involved on task forces or committees, working another 5 hours per month or 60 hours per year. That's a total of *210 hours.*

The total number of hours involved in the Community Educator's work comes to 1,384 hours. Some planners will tell you that, once you have made your best time estimate, it is wise to add 25% or, in this case, an additional 520 hours making a total of *1,904 hours for the project year.* The reasoning is that things always take more time than you think and delays are inevitable. There are 2,080 hours in a work year. In the case of the Geta

Clinic, it appears wise to hire a full-time educator (100%) to reach 3,000 teens with an AIDS prevention program.

As the job is conceptualized, the educator will spend the first four to five months preparing to teach and making contacts with the schools, and the remaining seven months of the project year providing the actual service. The factors we have included in calculating the amount of time an educator would spend to reach 3,000 teens should follow the implementation activities fairly closely. These calculations will also be needed as you determine the cost of the project. Often, as the true extent of time and effort needed is revealed, the implementation activities or the objectives may need to be modified to conform to budget restrictions.

APPENDIX B

Funding Resource Information

Listed below are common sources of information on funding resources that you might find helpful. This is a selective listing; for a more complete picture of funding opportunities, you can consult your local library or contact one of the following organizations or Web sites:

Grants, Etc.

This University of Michigan Web site, offering access to founding sources, in-kind resources, electronic journals, how-to guides, and other valuable resources, is located at http://www.ssw.umich.edu/grantsetc.

The Grantsmanship Center
   1125 W. Sixth Street, Fifth Floor
   PO Box 17220
   Los Angeles, CA 90017
   http://www.tgci.com

This organization has an extensive inventory of funding information, publishes a newspaper for grant-seeking organizations, and conducts national training on proposal writing and other areas of human service administration.

The Foundation Center
   79 Fifth Ave.
   New York, NY 10003
   http://foundationcenter.org

This independent, national service organization, established by foundations to provide an authoritative source of information on private philanthropic giving, publishes various directories and guides on foundations and has established a national network of reference collections through local and university libraries, community foundations, and nonprofit organizations.

INTERNET ADDRESSES OF SELECTED
FEDERAL AND STATE FUNDERS

Catalog of Federal Domestic Assistance: http://12.46.245.173/cfda/cfda.html

Grants.gov: http://www.grants.gov

U.S. Department of Housing and Urban Development (HUD) Grants: http://www.hud.gov/grants/

National Institutes of Health (NIH): http://www.nih.gov

Substance Abuse & Mental Health Services Administration: http://www.samhsa.gov

U.S. Department of Health & Human Services: http://www.dhhs.gov

U.S. Department of Education: http://www.ed.gov

MAJOR PUBLICATIONS

Annual Register of Grant Support. Marquis Who's Who, 4300 W. 62nd St., Indianapolis, IN 46206

Catalog of Federal Domestic Assistance. Superintendent of Documents, U.S. Government Printing Office, Washington, DC 20402

Federal Grants and Contracts Weekly. Capitol Publications, 1300 N. 17th St., Arlington, VA 22209

Federal Register. Superintendent of Documents, U.S. Government Printing Office, Washington, DC 20402

Foundation Directory, Foundation Directory Supplements, Foundation Grants Index, National Data Book of Foundations, National Guide to Funding for Children, Youth and Families, Corporate Foundation Profiles. Publications of the Foundation Center, 79 Fifth Ave., New York, NY 10003

Fund Raiser's Guide to Human Service Funding (2nd ed.). Taft Group, 5130 MacArthur Blvd. NW, Washington, DC 20016-3316

Grantsmanship Book. Reprints from The Grantsmanship Center, 1125 W. Sixth Street, Fifth Floor, P O Box 17220, Los Angeles, CA 90017

COMPUTERIZED SEARCHES AND DATABASES

A number of computerized search services are available that provide funding resource information. The advantage of such databases is that they can subdivide and index the funding information into a range of subjects and categories (e.g., by subject, by geographic area). Costs vary, and some of the information overlaps among different databases. Check your local university library for more information about search services. (Library tip: If you are no longer a student and want to use a university library, check to see if they have a "Friends of the Library" program. You may be able to join the library for a reasonable annual amount through this fundraising arm of the library.)

DIALOG Information Retrieval Service (http://www.dialog.com/products/productline/dialog.shtml) is among the largest databases covering a broad range of topics. Among the funding-related databases in the service are the following:

Federal Register abstracts: http://www.gpoaccess.gov/fr/index.html

Federal Research in Progress: http://library.dialog.com/bluesheets/html/bl0266.html

Foundation Directory: http://fconline.fdncenter.org

Foundation Grants Index: http://library.dialog.com/bluesheets/html/bl0027.html

Computerized searches are also useful for readily identifying literature and data for the needs/problem statement section of the proposal. One might find journal articles or other educational resources at the following search sites:

PsycINFO database: http://www.apa.org/psycinfo/

Education Resources Information Center (ERIC): http://www.eric.ed.gov

Wilson Social Science Abstracts: http://library.dialog.com/bluesheets/html/bl0142.html

Medline: http://www.ncbi.nlm.nih.gov/entrez/query.fcgi?DB=pubmed

LexisNexis: http://www.lexisnexis.com

ONLINE JOURNALS AND NEWSLETTERS

Chronicle of Philanthropy: http://www.philanthropy.com
Grantsmanship Center Magazine: http://www.tgci.com/magazine.shtml

REFERENCES AND SUGGESTED READINGS

Berk, R. A., & Rossi, P. H. (1990). *Thinking about program evaluation*. Newbury Park, CA: Sage.

Brewer, E., Achilles, C., Fuhriman, J., & Hollingsworth, C. (2001). *Finding funding: Grantwriting from start to finish, including project management and Internet use* (4th ed.). Thousand Oaks, CA: Corwin.

Bryce, H. J. (1987). *Financial and strategic management for nonprofit organizations*. Englewood Cliffs, NJ: Prentice-Hall.

Burke, M. A. (2002). *Simplified grantwriting*. Thousand Oaks, CA: Corwin.

Carlson, M. (2002). *Winning grants step by step* (2nd ed.). San Francisco, CA: Jossey-Bass.

Center for the Study of Social Policy. (1995). *Finding the data: A start-up list of outcome measures with annotations*. Washington, DC: Improved Outcomes for Children Project.

Connell, J., Kubisch, A., Schorr, L., & Weiss, C. (1995). *New approaches to evaluating community initiatives*. Washington, DC: Aspen Institute.

Diamond, H. (1998, Fall). A perfect union: Public-private partnerships can provide valuable services. *National Parks Forum, 40*, 4.

Dluhy, M., & Kravitz, S. (1990). *Building coalitions in the human services*. Newbury Park, CA: Sage.

Friedman, M. (2005). *Trying hard is not good enough: How to produce measurable improvements for customers and communities*. Victoria, BC: Trafford.

Gardner, S. (1999). *Beyond collaboration to results: Hard choices in the future of services to children and families*. Fullerton, CA: Center for Collaboration for Children and Arizona Prevention Resource Center.

Grace, K. S. (1997). *Beyond fundraising: New strategies for non-profit innovation and investment*. New York: John Wiley.

Harvard Family Research Project. (1996). *The evaluation exchange: Emerging strategies in evaluating child and family services*. Cambridge, MA: Harvard Family Research Project.

Joyaux, S. P. (1997). *Strategic fund development: Building profitable relationships that last*. Gaithersburg, MD: Aspen.

Kerney, C. A. (2005, June). Inside the mind of a grant reader. *Technology and Learning, 25*, 11.

Kettner, P. M., & Martin, L. L. (1996). *Measuring the performance of human service programs.* Thousand Oaks, CA: Sage.

Kettner, P. M., Moroney, R. K., & Martin, L. L. (1990). *Designing and managing programs.* Newbury Park, CA: Sage.

Kiritz, N. J. (1980). *Program planning and proposal writing.* Los Angeles: Grantsmanship Center.

Kniffel, L. (1995, November). Corporate sponsorship: The new direction in fundraising. *American Libraries, 26,* 10.

Krueger, R. A. (1994). *Focus groups: A practical guide for applied research* (2nd ed.). Thousand Oaks, CA: Sage.

Lauffer, A. (1997). *Grants, etc.* Thousand Oaks, CA: Sage.

Maxwell, D. J. (2005, February). Money, money, money: Taking the pain out of grant writing. *Teacher Librarian, 32,* 3.

Melaville, A. (1997). *A guide to selecting results and indicators: Implementing results-based budgeting.* Washington, DC: Finance Project.

National Institute for Dispute Resolution. (1997, January). What cultural groups face when being evaluated. *Forum, 32.*

Netting, F. E., & Williams, F. G. (1997). Is there an afterlife? How to move towards self-sufficiency when foundation dollars end. *Nonprofit Management & Leadership, 7,* 3.

Peterson, S. (2001). *The grantwriter's Internet companion: A resource for educators and others seeking grants and funding.* Thousand Oaks, CA: Corwin.

Pietrzak, J., Rabler, M., Renner, T., Ford, L., & Gilbert, N. (1990). *Practical program evaluation.* Newbury Park, CA: Sage.

Roth, J., Brooks-Gunn, J., Murray, L., & Foster, W. (1998). Promoting healthy adolescents: Synthesis of youth development program evaluations. *Journal of Research on Adolescence, 8,* 4, 423–459.

Ruskin, K., & Achilles, C. (1995). *Grantwriting, fundraising, and partnerships: Strategies that work!* Thousand Oaks, CA: Corwin.

Schaefer, M. (1985). *Designing and implementing procedures for health and human services.* Beverly Hills, CA: Sage.

Schaefer, M. (1987). *Implementing change in service programs.* Newbury Park, CA: Sage.

Schorr, L. (1995). *The case for shifting to results-based accountability.* Washington, DC: Center for the Study of Social Policy.

Schram, B. (1997). *Creating small scale social programs: Planning, implementation, and evaluation.* Thousand Oaks, CA: Sage.

United Way of America. (1996). *Measuring program outcomes: A practical approach* (4th ed.). Alexandria, VA: Author.

Vinter, R. D., & Kish, R. K. (1984). *Budgeting for not-for-profit organizations.* New York: Free Press.

Wacht, R. F. (1984). *Financial management in non-profit organizations.* Atlanta: Georgia State University.

W. K. Kellogg Foundation. (2004). *Logic model development guide.* Battle Creek, MI: Author.

Young, N., Gardner, S., & Coley, S. (1994). Getting to outcomes in integrated delivery models. In National Center for Service Integration (Ed.), *Making a difference: Moving to outcome-based accountability for comprehensive service reforms* (Resource Brief No. 7, chap. 2). Falls Church, VA: National Center for Service Integration.

PERFORMANCE INDICATORS

Accreditation Council on Services for People with Disabilities. (1993). *Outcome based performance measures: A procedures manual.* Towson, MD: Author.

Conoly, J., & Impara, J. *Mental measurements yearbook* (12th ed.). Lincoln, NE: Buros Institute of Mental Measurements.

Department of Health and Human Services. *Performance Measurement in Selected Public Health Programs* (1995–1996 Regional Meeting Report). Washington, DC: Public Health Service.

KIDS COUNT data book: State profiles of child well-being. (1995). Baltimore: Annie E. Casey Foundation.

Kumfer, K., Shur, G., Ross, J., Bunnell, K., Librett, J., & Millward, A. (1993). *Measurement in prevention: A manual on selecting and using instruments to evaluate prevention programs.* Washington, DC: U.S. Department of Health and Human Services, Center for Substance Abuse Prevention.

Magura, S., & Moses, B. (1986). *Outcome measures for child welfare services.* Washington, DC: Child Welfare League of America.

Touliatos, J., Perlmutter, B., & Straus, M. (1990). *Handbook of family measurement techniques.* Newbury Park, CA: Sage.

U.S. Department of Health and Human Services. (1994). *Assessing drug abuse among adolescents and adults: Standardized instruments* (Clinical Report Series). Rockville, MD: Public Health Service, National Institute on Drug Abuse.

Weiss, H., & Jacobs, F. (1988). *Evaluating family programs.* New York: Aldine de Gruyter.

INDEX

ABOUT THE AUTHORS

Soraya M. Coley, PhD, is the Provost and Vice President for Academic Affairs at California State University, Bakersfield. She has more than 25 years of academic and administrative experience as well as extensive community service. She served as Provost and Vice President for Academic Affairs at Alliant International University and as Dean of the College of Human Development and Community Service at California State University, Fullerton.

Cynthia A. Scheinberg, PhD, is a licensed clinical psychologist with more than 20 years of administrative management in nonprofit agencies. She has served as the Executive Director of the Coalition for Children, Adolescents, and Parents (CCAP) in Orange, California and as Senior Vice President of Clinical Services for Anka Behavioral Health, Inc., and she is currently the Executive Director of New Connections in Concord, California. She has a doctorate in clinical psychology from Pacifica Graduate Institute in Santa Barbara, California, and a master's degree in cultural anthropology from California State University, Fullerton.